MOOO116838

TO LEAD AS JESUS LED

ERIC G. STEPHAN AND R. WAYNE PACE

CFI,
SPRINGVILLE, UTAH

ISBN 13: 978-1-55517-993-9
ISBN 10: 1-55517-993-2

Published by CFI, an imprint of Cedar Fort, Inc., 2373 W. 700 S., Springville, UT, 84663
Distributed by Cedar Fort, Inc., www.cedarfort.com

LIBRARY OF CONGRESS CATALOGING-IN-PUBLICATION DATA

Stephan, Eric G.
    To lead as Jesus led / Eric Stephan and R. Wayne Pace.
        p. cm.
    Includes bibliographical references and index.
    ISBN-13: 978-1-55517-993-9
    1. Leadership--Religious aspects--Christianity. 2. Jesus Christ--Leadership. 3. Church of Jesus Christ of Latter-day Saints--Doctrines. 4. Mormon Church--Doctrines. I. Pace, R. Wayne. II. Title.

    BV4597.53.L43S74 2006
    253--dc22

                          2006032413

Cover design by Nicole Williams
Cover design © 2006 by Lyle Mortimer
Typeset by Angela Olsen

Printed in the United States of America

10   9   8   7   6   5   4   3   2   1

Printed on acid-free paper

TO LEAD AS
JESUS LED

DEDICATION

To our splendid wives,
Sandra Utley Stephan and Gae Tueller Pace,
and a bunch of remarkable children

TABLE OF CONTENTS

ACKNOWLEDGMENTS

To all of those who have urged us to write about leadership, we express our immense gratitude. We want you to know that we approached this task with considerable fear and trembling, yet with excitement about the opportunity to think in new ways and to walk over previously uncharted ground to find a more effective approach to successful leadership. We have been awed, inspired, and instructed as we examined the life of Jesus as a perfect model of correct principles of leadership. We have been changed by this experience, and we now teach and counsel in new ways. Through these pages we share our personal testimony of Jesus Christ—that he lives and invites all to "come unto me," "learn of me," "follow me."

Most important, as individuals writing constantly and erratically, we express our profound appreciation to our two spouses; they provided the support and necessary sustenance to complete this work. We salute you, Sandra Utley Stephan and Gae Tueller Pace. Bear with us! We may do this again.

In Search of the Best Leadership Approach

Some of life's greatest personal leadership challenges are caused by small crises at home, church, or at work, when a young person or another adult needs to be influenced or re-directed in a positive way. All too often we compound the problem and make the situation worse because we get caught up in the heat of the moment or simply fail to follow correct principles and Christlike perspectives when we attempt to lead and influence others. Even when we stay reasonably calm, some of us have lingering doubts about the way in which we tried to handle those little and big, even gigantic, crises, and we frequently ask, what should I have done differently?

Whether we want to be or not, all of us are leaders. Whenever we influence others toward a goal, we are acting as leaders. Whether we intend to or not, we interact with others and we influence them. Our influence is the greatest part of our leadership. We have been leaders in the past and we will continue to be leaders in the future. Leadership is not necessarily a function of a specific work position, family role, or church calling. It is a way of getting work done and handling responsibilities. Indeed, leadership may even be considered a way of life.

Each of us has so many opportunities to lead and influence others in our homes, at our places of employment, and in the church and community, that the only consideration before us should be: How can we improve our leadership performance? How can we increase our influence in those situations where individuals are looking for guidance and direction?

Leadership acts touch upon so many aspects of our daily lives that the leadership process often eludes direct and accurate analysis. Both layman and scholars alike question the nature of this elusive process. Why do certain individuals attract such loyal followers and have such a strong influence over others? Can leaders be efficient without using raw power and authority? Is it possible to use the same principles of leadership at home as well as in the workplace? And which leadership style is the most effective?

Leadership is attributed to many different causes: kingly bloodlines, personality traits, specific actions, impelling circumstances that raise people to the occasion, and various combinations of all of the above.

What We Knew

We have been concerned with the scholarly study of leadership for over thirty years. We have read, researched, and written about leadership. We have discussed, analyzed, and dissected the subject with friends, students, colleagues, and relatives. We have pondered the topic in church meetings, in university classrooms, and in the hallways and walkways of hotels, cities, libraries, and offices.

We knew that effective leaders were, above everything else, men and women of action who attract followers to a cause or an idea. We found ourselves in total agreement with President James E. Faust when he said that, "A good leader expects much, inspires greatly, and sets on fire those he is called to lead. Now, a leader must cause things to happen and lives to be affected. Something should move and change" (*Ensign*, November 1980, 34).

Leaders sense problems and initiate actions to resolve them. Yet it seemed like every book we read failed to capture the excitement of such a simple idea. When trying to find the principles that produce delightful leadership, we were confronted mostly with lists and discussions of abstract concepts and uninspiring leadership techniques. Interestingly, we also noticed that most books about how to lead and influence others had a rather short shelf life, quickly collected dust, and were discarded. Those that were marginally helpful frequently suggested approaches that were sometimes uncomfortable to use because they seemed unnatural, concerned more with control then with freedom, were manipulative, and did not meet the genuine needs of others.

Searching the Scriptures

When we turned to the scriptures, we found what we had been fruitlessly searching for: the simple, essential principles that produce real leadership. We found treasures of knowledge in reading and pondering the scriptural accounts of the ways Jesus led people and raised them to their highest potential.

To our astonishment, we found, from these scriptural accounts, that the language of Jesus favored "inviting and helping" people to participate in exciting activities, rather than delegating and controlling them in an effort to get them to do something they were not much inclined to do in the first place. Jesus invited, encouraged, and helped people accomplish tasks, rather than simply telling them what to do.

When someone unexpectedly made a mistake, rather than reprimanding them, as many leadership texts suggest, Jesus was much more inclined to redirect their behavior in a positive way through clarifying the goals to be achieved and the rewards that could be received by following a better path. Amazing, also, is the fact that while leadership scholars and writers struggle to define the relationship that should exist between a leader and followers, Jesus demonstrated and clearly stated the most effective way to relate to co-workers, neighbors, church, and family members so as to have a magnificent influence for good in their lives.

Indeed, there are so many things to be said about the Jesus' incredible approach to powerful and positive leadership that no single book or article could begin to explain the skills and attributes that he demonstrated so perfectly in his life. However, we will point out a few of the skills and attributes that we discovered when studying Christ's remarkable leadership approach. Emulating these same skills and attributes will allow you to succeed in a lasting way as an effective leader.

Jesus Shows the Way

It becomes increasingly clear when studying the life of Christ that leadership, in its finest form, is much more than telling people what to do—a means of imposing one's ideas and will upon others. Jesus is considered by Christians to be the greatest leader ever to walk the earth. For the master leader, leadership is characterized by a willingness to serve, rather than be served. Jesus did not emphasize the authority of a ruler-leader, but the humility of a servant-leader.

Jesus said many times, "Come, follow me," and continued to explain: "I am among you as he that serveth" (Luke 22:27). His approach to leadership stressed "do what I do" rather than "do what I say." He walked and worked among his followers, listening to their needs, responding lovingly and making no harsh demands on others to satisfy his own desires.

In the Doctrine and Covenants the Lord warns:

We have learned by sad experience that it is the nature and disposition of almost all men, as soon as they get a little authority as they suppose, they will immediately begin to exercise unrighteous dominion. Hence many are called, but few are chosen.

No power or influence can or ought to be maintained by virtue of the priesthood, only by persuasion, by long-suffering, by gentleness and meekness, and by love unfeigned: By kindness and pure knowledge, which shall greatly enlarge the soul without hypocrisy, and without guile (D&C 121:39–42).

Avoiding unrighteous dominion and following the Savior's leadership example is not easy, but it can be done. President N. Eldon Tanner, a great church and business leader, suggested that "In order to lead as Jesus led, we are faced with many challenges. One of the first steps in meeting these challenges is to realize that Christ is a model of correct leadership; and, as the scriptures record his life and teachings, they become case studies of divine leadership" (Tanner, 1977, 4).

As we consider the scriptures and their case studies, the most dominant features of Christ's leadership become evident in the Savior's efforts to influence and support his followers.

Emulate His Attributes

As a Prophet and great leader, President Spencer W. Kimball explained to a group of potentially great leaders, "I make no apology for giving something of the accomplishments of Jesus Christ to those who seek success as leaders. If we would be eminently successful, here is our pattern All the ennobling, perfect, and beautiful qualities of maturity, of strength, and of courage are found in this one person. As a large, surly mob, armed to the teeth, came to take him prisoner, he faced them resolutely and said, 'Whom seek ye?'

The mob, startled, mumbled his name, 'Jesus of Nazareth.'

'I am he,' answered Jesus of Nazareth with pride and courage—and with power: the soldiers 'went backward, and fell to the ground.'

A second time he said, 'Whom seek ye?' and when they named him, he said, 'I have told you that I am he: if therefore ye seek me, let these [his disciples] go their way'" (Kimball, 1979, 5).

A thorough reading of Christ's daily activities as reported in the Gospels depicts Jesus as a man who was creative, persistent, confident, and of "good cheer." He enjoyed mingling with people and children. He loved crowds and yet he found quiet moments when he could be alone.

Jesus never panicked. There are no scriptural accounts of Jesus living his life in quiet desperation or perpetual sadness. He was filled with light, truth, and joy. Truly, he is the Great Exemplar, worthy to be emulated in every way. It is a most comforting thought to believe that we are a little like the Savior and that he is a little like us.

Unlocking Powerful Leadership

Throughout this book are the words, "keys." Keys open locks and disclose what is inside a room or a chest. Keys are also considered guides, solutions, and explanations to unlock a mystery or something that may be difficult to explain.

The attributes that Jesus possessed that attracted people to him, and the leadership principles he used to encourage his followers to action, comprise the quintessential keys to his perfect leadership. Identifying these keys helps us to understand how to lead as the Savior led.

Five simple yet powerful leadership keys, exemplified in the life of Christ, are elaborated upon in the following pages. The fact that these keys are specific and quite easily understood gives encouragement to some of us who may dislike being formally appointed to positions of leadership, or who are a little intimidated by the problems associated with being the leader.

These same fundamental keys give guidance to those who are called to be leaders, or who want to help others become good leaders. Additionally, these same keys give considerable guidance to parents when working with their children. Furthermore, these simple but powerful keys gives positive and clear direction to those who feel a need to have a greater influence with others at work and in the community.

Today, the world is desperately in need of selfless, Christlike leadership. The rapid growth of the Church requires faithful men and women to assume leadership roles at every level. Exemplary leadership in business, industry, and government is sought after and generously rewarded. Families need to be unified and young people strengthened against unscrupulous enticements. Thus, more effective leadership in the home is absolutely essential.

President David O. McKay has described what can happen as we look to the Savior to meet such leadership challenges: "What you sincerely think in your heart of Christ will determine what you are, will largely determine what your acts will be. No person can study his divine personality, can accept his teachings, or follow his example, without becoming conscious of an uplifting and refining influence within himself" (McKay, 1969, 411).

We are, now, quite confident that the answer to the question "Which of all the current leadership theories most closely resembles the way in which Christ led others?" can be given with unequivocal certainty, "None of them!"

The thousands of different theories, skills, and attitudes that are called "vital for becoming a better leader" can all be synthesized into one man, Jesus Christ.

"One of the great teachings of the Man of Galilee, the Lord Jesus Christ, was that you and I carry within us immense possibilities. In urging us to be perfect as our Father in Heaven is perfect, Jesus was not taunting us or teasing us. He was telling us a great truth about our possibilities and potentials. It is a truth almost too stunning to contemplate" (Kimball, 1979, 7).

Knowing now where to look for the correct approach to successful leadership, let us go forward, together, to examine the life of Christ as a demonstration of five quintessential keys to effective leadership, and see if we can catch a glimpse of the extraordinary adventure of perfect leadership and its challenge for all of us.

> We can see and understand only a little about God now, as if we were peering at His reflection in a poor mirror: but someday we are going to see Him in His completeness, face to face. (*Reach Out*, 1967, 422)

1

THE FIRST KEY:
TREAT OTHERS AS FRIENDS

Supper ended.

The disciples shifted and moved to find comfortable places.

Jesus rose, poured water into a basin, and began to wash the disciples' feet.

After Jesus had washed their feet and sat down again, he asked:

> Know ye what I have done to you? Ye call me Master and Lord . . . If I then, your Lord and Master, have washed your feet; ye also ought to wash one another's feet. For I have given you an example, that ye should do as I have done to you. (John 13:12–15)

Then Christ gave his disciples the key to understand the relationship that should exist between leaders and their followers:

> Henceforth I call you not servants; for the servant knoweth not what his lord doeth: but I have called you friends; for all things that I have heard of my Father I have made known unto you. (John 15:15)

Great leaders try to replace the master/servant and superior/subordinate relationship with a more trusting, friend-to-friend association. If Christ is to be our leader, we must be his friend. If we are his friends, we will follow him. In modern scriptures, Christ explains that "it is expedient that I give unto you this commandment, that ye become even as my friends in days when I was with them" (D&C 84:77).

If we want to follow him, we must become his friends. To become a friend is to become an ally, to unite and join together for a specific purpose. As one may surmise, the penetrating question concerns how Christ, beyond giving a commandment, encouraged followers and strangers to become his friends.

Christ's leadership style is intimately interwoven with his admonition to become a friend. The first essential key to becoming a leader like the man called Jesus is to treat others as friends.

What Is a Friend?

The King James Version of the New Testament was translated out of the original Greek. In the Greek language the word "friend" means equal. If we are equal it means that we are the same as another in value and degree. Jesus emphasized that a servant doesn't know what his Master is doing. And then quickly added "but I have called you friends; for all things that I have heard of my Father I have made known unto you."

The original Greek language indicates that the word "friend" also means "from the same family." Being from the same family means that family members are a group; a group that is descended from a common progenitor and whose members are closely related to each other. It is not difficult to understand from the language Jesus used and the activities in which he engaged that Jesus was establishing sound and trusting relationships with those whom he sought to influence and lead.

Synonyms for the word friend chart the landscape of the territory covered by the idea of being a friend. A friend is an acquaintance, a comrade, a companion, a chum, a confidant, a partner, a buddy, a pal, a sidekick, a crony, a cohort, and a consort. A friend is also a patron, supporter, backer, benefactor, a well-wisher, an encourager, an advocate, a defender, a partisan, and an adherent. In addition, friends are referred to as allies, colleagues, associates, brothers, and followers.

The word "friendship" and its synonyms sketch the features that characterize a friend. For example, friendship means having a good feeling, friendliness, harmony, accord, amicableness, consonance, understanding, sympathy, good fellowship, cordiality, neighborliness, and goodwill.

A "friendly" person is one who is kindly, helpful, well-disposed, amiable, neighborly, amicable, loving, familiar, affectionate, kind-hearted, cordial, genial, warmhearted, ardent, devoted, sympathetic, gracious, generous, chummy, companionable, convivial, hospitable, social, accessible, and affable.

Leadership as "the creation of friends" is such a profound concept that it turns commonsense definitions of leadership on their heads.

Leadership as exemplified by Jesus is quite different from the common way leadership is typically exercised. We usually think of leadership as influencing others through interpersonal communication; we usually think of the leader as the most influential person in the group. Leading people connotes that someone is out in front and others are behind. Great leaders are those who take charge, who motivate people, who set goals, and who direct people toward accomplishing the goals. Many associate the concept of leadership with people who boss, command, guide, blaze trails, wheel, deal, and seize the reins.

The popular concept of leading implies being the head, supreme, great, preeminent, unrivaled, unparalleled, stellar, and topmost. Slang phrases indicate how some people think about a leader: bigwig, king-pin, magnate, mogul, tycoon, and godfather.

A dramatic contrast is evident between the meaning of friend and the popular meaning of leader! Friends have a long and abiding mature love for one another. They sacrifice for one another; they do for one another what each would do for the other. One is not superior nor the other subordinate; one is not leader while the other follows; they are true and authentic brothers and sisters, equal in each other's sight.

Friends are generous and hospitable with one another. They are devoted and genial, happy to be in the presence of each other. They are willing to place the needs of the other ahead of their own. One of the greatest stories of friendship ever recorded is that of Damon and Pythias.

Pythias was thrown into prison for an offense against the King. Because Pythias was married and had a family, Damon offered to take his place in prison, while Pythias went home to say goodbye to his family. The King was so impressed by the offer that he agreed to the arrangement, provided Damon was to suffer death in Pythias' place if Pythias failed to return. Damon accepted the plan.

At the appointed hour, Pythias had not arrived and Damon was taken to the place of execution. Just as Damon was to be put to death, Pythias returned and took his place. The King was so taken by the fact that Pythias would return to have his life taken in order to keep his promise to Damon that the King released them both.

The total commitment of Damon and Pythias to one another is characteristic of true friendship. These friends symbolize, in an earthly way, the heavenly and divine friendship of Christ with his disciples and members of his Church. Complete and total willingness to accept the burdens of others is the fullness of friendship toward which we are striving as leaders when we follow Christ's example.

The Power of a Friend-to-Friend Bond

Leadership as a friend-to-friend bond, warranted by a resolute determination to fulfill a sacred vow, is the challenge we are seeking to accept and achieve. When a friend-to-friend relationship elicits a pledge, resolution, and decision to stand for others, to do their bidding, and to raise them in stature and character, this illustrates the kind of leadership exemplified by the man called Jesus.

To have a person in a position of responsibility say that we are his friends is a thrilling and strengthening experience. To feel and know that someone loves us, believes in us, trusts us, and expects good things from us are inspiring. Pure, powerful, loving friendship binds people to one another.

The first step toward strengthening your own leadership style is to cultivate strong friendships. People follow those whom they like; they like their friends. We go along with our friends. Friendship creates a willingness to follow.

Friendship establishes the foundation upon which leadership can be exercised. You cannot lead an enemy. You can lead friends!

Friendship not only makes leadership possible, but it also makes influencing others more effective and much easier to achieve. It is easier to invite friends to be involved. It is easier to want to serve a friend. It is easier to be committed to a friend. We are encouraged more easily by friends.

The very nature of friendship—as a feeling of loving, personal, helpful, kind, and dedicated associates—fulfills the deep longing all of us have for someone with whom we can share and grow.

"Among life's sweetest blessings," said President David O. McKay, "is fellowship with men and women whose ideals and aspirations are high and noble. Next to a sense of kinship with God comes the helpfulness, encouragement, and inspiration of friends. Friendship is a sacred possession. . . . To live, laugh, love one's friends, and be loved by them is to bask in the sunshine of life" (McKay, 1953, 253).

The Prophet Joseph Smith stated that friendship is one of the "grand fundamental principles of Mormonism." He described friendship as like Brother Trulin in his blacksmith's shop welding iron-to-iron; "it unites the human family with its happy influence" (Smith, 1938, 316).

You can be a leader, of course, without being or having a friend; but you will have chosen the more difficult route. Being a friend is the simpler, easier, more effective way to achieve Christlike leadership. Being a friend opens the door to exciting, moving, powerful leadership, without the use of complex, lengthy strategies for winning and influencing people. By being a friend, and having a friend, you have the basis for great leadership.

Friendship is both universal and imperative for leadership, because it applies to both the temporal and spiritual aspects of leading. Friendship transcends this temporary existence and flows over into eternity.

Friendship provides the energy for Christ's effective leadership. It can also be the basis of our leadership effectiveness. That does not mean that we can avoid all other approaches to leadership, but leadership techniques are wholly less effective when we are not working with friends. These methods are fully more effective when we are working with friends. The number and complexity of leadership techniques can be measurably reduced when we begin with the assumption of friendship.

A father of seven beautiful children announced, during a recent sacrament meeting talk, that he had been a father and parent for thirty-five years, but that he did not want to continue in that capacity anymore. He explained that he had observed how wonderfully his children treated their friends. He noticed that they spent hours on the phone talking to their friends. They dreamed together and defended each other, and enjoyed being together for long periods of time.

The father said that he would rather be treated like a friend than a parent. Serious faces turned into smiles as the audience began to chuckle and to nod their approval of the idea.

The father, feeling that he was getting his point across, then looked directly at his wife and announced that he did not want to be her husband anymore. Briefly he recounted their several years of exciting courtship. Apparently they spent much time together talking about the future, present, and past. Together they learned how to dance and play tennis. They were also proud of each other, defended each other, and spoke frequently on the telephone.

Above all, the father said, "I treated my sweetheart as my best friend. She was my best friend. And I believe that I would rather be her best friend again."

Maybe he was trying to explain that friendship precedes great fatherhood and great motherhood, or maybe he was trying to suggest that in marriage, romance decreases but a friendship lasts forever.

Friendship also precedes great leadership. It may be that other leadership theories are less effective because they are based on the assumption that people are not and can never be friends. Thus they provide weaker, more complex methods for leading.

In front of a crackling fire in Vail, Colorado, a small group of successful business leaders was considering the subject of executive leadership. One executive introduced the idea that it might be possible to lead with love, and to be friends with employees and even competitors. A hearty laugh filled the room, and a rush of comments quickly followed. "Are you kidding?" one person shouted out. "You would immediately be labeled a pushover and a soft negotiator. You'd be annihilated and probably bankrupt in less than six months." Others agreed.

The thought that leading others can be made more effective and easier by operating on the fundamental principle of friendship was discussed no further that evening. It almost seemed as though the rough and tough approach to leadership had won out. Yet strangely everyone in the room was trying to be friendly. Maybe they were hearing the quiet supplication of the Man from Galilee saying, "Love one another," urging them to be friends with one another.

Friendship built on a true concern for the other person must not be interpreted as a soft acquiescence to their problems or to mediocre performance.

On the contrary, a good friend would tell a close companion in need, "I understand," not "I agree with what you are doing or the way you are handling the situation." A friend does not spend much time wallowing around in self-pity, but asks, "What can we do to improve the situation?"

The consummate relationship to be realized for leading and influencing others effectively is that of friend-to-friend. Thus the first-essential key to a more natural and less threatening way to lead is to treat others as friends.

How to Treat Someone as a Friend

In a leadership seminar, a businessman asked, "But how do you treat someone as a friend?" The facilitator conducted an interesting exercise in order to answer the participant's question. He asked everyone in the room to close their eyes and imagine a long hallway. "Now, imagine that one of your good friends has been away on a trip for two weeks," he said. "As you look up from your end of the hallway, imagine that your friend just came into view from the other end of the hallway. See yourself and your friend walking toward each other and stopping to face each other. Watch what you do and say."

Then the seminar leader asked the participants to explain what they said and did when they met their friends in the hallway. "I smiled and talked enthusiastically about where she had been and what she had been doing," said one woman. "We laughed and hugged," said another. "I asked if he needed any help and suggested that he come over to supper that evening so that we could talk longer," said a man.

After numerous responses, the message became quite clear: Treat others as you treat your best friends. Say hello. Smile. Ask questions that express your interest in them. Ask what they are doing. Express appreciation for them. Be of service. Encourage them. And don't be afraid to walk, work, eat, and dream together.

For many adults and children, it's easier to talk to a friend than a parent or a boss. That can be a great advantage for you if you have established a friend to friend relationship with those over whom you have some responsibility.

When we treat others as friends we boost their dignity and feelings of self worth. This is especially true when we are perceived as someone in authority. The quickest way to help others feel valued and of great worth is to ask their opinions about an important matter and listen to their answers. Friends listen to each other and feel a desire to help each other.

Our relationship with others is strengthened when we eliminate words like "I", "Me", and "Mine" from our vocabulary. Notice how carefully you avoid hurting a friend by avoiding strong negative comments and communicating in a positive way. Good friendships usually include exciting communication exchanges that frequently include the words "we," "our," and "us." Someone said that our mouths cause us more trouble than any other part of us. And it's true that when we criticize, and make demeaning comments to others, relationships are weakened and sometimes destroyed. Jesus warned us that, "whatsoever entereth in at the mouth goeth into the belly, and is cast out into the draught? But those things which proceed out of the mouth come forth from the heart; and they defile the man" (Matt: 15:17–18). Messages of hope and optimism strengthen the bonds of friendship.

When President Spencer W. Kimball visited prisoners in the Utah state prison, observers noted that he shook hands, asked questions, made positive comments, and generally did not distinguish between greeting a group of Priesthood holders and incarcerated convicts. The prisoners responded wonderfully well and ask President Kimball if they could have their picture taken with him. He treated them as his brothers and his friends. Most were deeply moved and impressed by this prophet from Salt Lake City.

Since we already know how we treat our best friends, it is not too difficult to make the shift to treating others as good friends. If it convenient for you, we suggest that you stop reading for a moment, relax, and think about how you do treat your best friends? Like the father who noticed how his children treated their friends, what do you do to strengthen your relationship with your best friends? Are you are doing similar things with your own children, with Church members, and with fellow workers? If you are like the rest of us, you'll be able to quickly identify some things that you can do to increase the strength of your friendship with others. Maximizing this first fundamental key—to treat others as friends—is well worth a little of your time and energy. This is such a simple but profound concept that it is no wonder that Jesus instituted this principle with his early followers.

Love Does Not Fail

What general attitude underlies a radiant friend-to-friend relationship? The answer is simple and is available to all of us. Genuine friendship is fired, fueled, driven, motivated, and made real by LOVE!

In both ancient and modern scriptures, we read the clear call to follow by reason of love. "If ye love me, keep my commandments" (John 14:15). Not, "If you know what's good for you, you will do what I say."

If we were to ask the Prophet Nephi, "What is the most desirable thing that we could receive from God?" what would his answer be?

In receiving an interpretation of his father's dream, an angel said to Nephi:

> Behold the Lamb of God, yea even the Son of the Eternal Father! Knowest thou the meaning of the tree which thy father saw?
>
> And I answered him saying: Yea, it is the love of God, which sheddeth itself abroad in the hearts of the children of men; wherefore, it is the most desirable above all things.
>
> And he spake unto me saying: Yea, and the most joyous to the soul. (I Nephi 11:21–23)

Love binds people together and unites them with the Divine. All things are easier to achieve when they are done for someone we love and respect. If we love and admire Jesus, we are able to follow him. Obligations are easier to keep and goals easier to achieve when they are sought in love.

Jesus demonstrated unabashed love toward the disciples when he washed their feet at the Last Supper. No thoughts of impropriety or humiliation entered his mind as he readied materials and knelt before each apostle.

Peter, however, was startled. To witness a divine person humble himself by washing the dust from the feet of his followers and toweling them dry created an unforgettable memory.

Even more astonishing to Peter was the later realization that Jesus did not hesitate to wash the feet of Judas who was in the very process of betraying Christ.

No doubt the early followers of Jesus learned that the line between Master and Servant must be obliterated. All must be served—the leper, orphan, widow, elderly, poor, and misguided.

After the washing, the conversation focused on the love of his followers, one for another. Little did they know that their close relationship with the Savior was drawing to an end.

Jesus spoke intimately but confidently. He concluded his final discourse with the most significant admonitions of his sacred ministry.

He began:

> Little children, yet a little while I am with you. You shall seek me; and as I said to the Jews: Whither I go you cannot come; so I say to you now. A new commandment I give unto you: that you love one another, as I have loved you, that you also love one another. By this shall all men know that you are my disciples, if you have love one for another. (John 13:33–35)

Jesus' demonstration of humility and love, by washing the feet of his disciples, was now being followed by the admonition to love one another, even as Jesus loved them.

These last urgings of Christ are significant because he did not intend them only for the Apostles, but for all of us (John 17:20–21). They remind us that love grows out of friendship.

Recently, Joe Moglia, former football coach and now Ameritrade CEO said that executive and leadership success requires "spiritual soundness, dedication, courage, and love." His interviewer asked: "Love? That's an unusual word in business." Mr. Moglia replied: "I define love as the willingness to sacrifice yourself for the betterment of someone else—the team, the organization" (USA Today, January 19, 2004, 4B). When we love someone we have, as President Gordon B. Hinckley said, "an anxious concern for their well-being and happiness." Jesus loved his followers and never said or did anything unless it was beneficial to their growth and happiness.

Create a friend-to-friend relationship and you also create the basis for true admiration, trust and regard. The purest, simplest, and most natural way to lead, influence, and positively impact others begins when we treat others as friends.

2

THE SECOND KEY:
CREATE A POSITIVE FORCE

The story of Jesus is the simple narrative of a young boy growing up in a humble family increasing in his abilities to teach and lead others, suffering disappointments and sorrow, and building such a strong following that his influence was only beginning at the time of his death. Christ's magnificent life and legacy comprise the greatest leadership model and success story of all time.

Jesus, like most of us, did not start at the top of a well developed organization, nor did he have wealthy and influential parents to assure him positions of power and influence in his community. Rather he grew up in Nazareth, a small town in the outlying province of Jerusalem. Even when reports spread that a new prophet-leader had arisen from that country town, the question was asked, with an air of derision, "Can any good thing come out of Nazareth?" (John 1:46)

Good things and good people, nevertheless, did come out of Nazareth. One of them, Jesus, manifested such energetic and incisive leadership skills that he affected people for thousands of years.

Christ's powerful leadership style is characterized by three central features: (1) strong commitment to the task at hand, (2) a great compassion for the people he led, and (3) a consistently encouraging attitude. These leadership attributes melded to produce a dynamic force that emanated from Christ and influenced his followers to act and become involved. They constitute an inner force and are, indeed, the very soul of authentic leadership.

Leading with Commitment

Rather early in his life, Jesus was given an opportunity to confirm his commitment to assuming a leadership role among his people. The scriptures record that after being in the wilderness for forty days without eating, Jesus was tempted three times by Satan, who said, "If thou be the Son of God, command this stone that it be made bread" (Luke 4:3).

This first challenge seems to urge Jesus to use his power to satisfy physical and material needs—to put temporal things ahead of spiritual things. He could satisfy his hunger immediately and then continue to achieve considerable material gain by abandoning his divine purpose and earthly ministry. He could use his inherent power for selfish reasons rather than service to others.

For the second challenge, Luke reports, Satan took Jesus up onto a high mountain, showed him all the kingdoms of the world, and said to him: "All this power will I give thee, and the glory of them: for that is delivered unto me; and to whomsoever I will I give it" (Luke 4:6). Jesus could partake of earthly splendor, power, and glory. He could give up his Messianic mission and gather considerable fame and fortune for himself.

In a third effort, Satan tempted Jesus to verify his Son-of-God relationship by suggesting that Jesus cast himself down from the pinnacle of the temple so that angels would bear Jesus up, "lest at any time thou dash thy foot against a stone" (Luke 4:11).

We are not certain whether Jesus was literally placed upon a high mountain top or not, but we do know that a temptation tests us and forces us to make a choice. We also know that temptations come directly from our own humanness and the world around us.

It is natural to desire recognition and reward for what we do. Sometimes, however, rewards are promised to us only if we agree to certain conditions. A girl may be asked to surrender certain liberties in return for a young man's undying devotion. A young man may be promised great monetary rewards if he deals in drugs. A businessman may be promised success if he engages in questionable or dishonest transactions.

Each of us must examine our choices from time to time to see if what we are sacrificing is really worth it. There is no question that temptations are real. If we resist and overcome them, we prove our worthiness to become friends and companions with those with whom we work.

Forty days and nights Jesus was in the wilderness. His experience may have been like your own moments of concern, when doubts enter your mind about accepting a position of leadership and responsibility.

Recently a faithful young mother was called to an important leadership responsibility in her stake. The anticipation of becoming acquainted with a new program, and trying to lead people, with whom she wasn't particularly well acquainted, was almost overwhelming.

To make matters worse, she was a single parent trying to raise a family, work, and go to school. You can imagine the struggle in her mind as she considered what might be gained by accepting the calling in contrast to what might be achieved at work or in school if she rejected the position. She could devote all of her time to other important aspects of her life.

This devoted woman, nevertheless, symbolically followed the humble man from Galilee into the wilderness and received confirmation to accept the calling. Christ and this woman are real people, in real places, reaching for vision, power, and confidence that are the very heart and soul of leadership.

Having achieved the assurance of his mission, Jesus put Satan's temptations behind him. Hence, he came away strengthened and fully committed. The scriptures record, "Jesus returned in the power of the Spirit into Galilee: and there went out a fame of him through all the region round about" (Luke 4:14).

After receiving such divine assurance, a humble leader can then go forward with absolute conviction and commitment that the course of action is the right course and is what the Savior would do in a similar situation.

Jesus' commitment became visible through a cause. Leaders commit themselves to a cause. But that is not enough. True leaders commit themselves to a *good* cause which becomes a purpose beyond the everyday activities of daily living. Great leaders become committed to great causes that become the focus of the leaders' constant and patient devotion.

If we ever dream of becoming great at anything, we might begin by asking ourselves, "Am I going to allow daily activities to govern my life, or am I going to live my life according to noble principles?" Unless you make a conscious decision to do more than engage in the routine necessities of daily living, your life will inevitably become shallow.

Though Jesus still had much growing to do, accompanied by further temptations (Luke 22:28), he clearly knew his purpose and goal. Unlike some of us who are uncertain about our goals and directions, and whether we are using our time and energy appropriately, Jesus acted and spoke with great authority, sincerity, and courage—magnifying his calling at every opportunity and bringing about positive changes in people's lives.

President Joseph F. Smith emphatically stated: "One of the highest qualities of all true leadership is a high standard of courage. . . . There has never been a time in the Church when its leaders were not required to be courageous men; not alone courageous in the sense that they were able to meet physical dangers, but also in the sense that they were steadfast and true to a clear and upright conviction" (*Gospel Doctrine*, fifth ed. [Salt Lake City: Deseret Book, 1939], 155).

Imagine how startled Nicodemus, an important man and a member of the Sanhedrin, must have been when Jesus boldly declared, "Verily, verily, I say unto thee, except a man be born again he cannot see the kingdom of God" (John 3:3).

Remember the rich man's surprise when Jesus advised him to sell all that he had and distribute it to the poor, so that he would have treasures in heaven. And then to come without hesitation and faithfully follow him (Matthew 19:16–22).

Jesus' cause was clear, and he pressed forward with daring ideas and powerful language.

Consider further the courage and determination derived from Jesus' commitment when he cleansed the temple of money changers, and how he answered the Pharisees' challenge to his authority!

Recall that the Pharisees prided themselves on their strict observance of the law and their overzealous belief in both written and oral religious tradition.

Jesus had just declared, "I am the light of the world: he that followeth me shall not walk in darkness, but shall have the light of life."

Almost lightening quick, the Pharisees responded with "Thou

bearest record of thyself; thy record is not true."

Without hesitation, Jesus replied, "Though I bear record of myself, yet my record is true: for I *know* whence I come, and whither I go" (John 8:12–14, emphasis added).

When accepting a leadership position you too must "study it out" in your mind and reflect on it. You can also alleviate some of your concerns by talking to someone who holds or has held a similar position. By asking for their help in learning how to perform more effectively in the new calling, you benefit greatly from their insight and experience.

New managers should sit down with their former counterparts and ask for information and advice. A new bishop, Relief Society president, secretary, clerk, teacher, in fact everyone who assumes a position of influence would do well to sit down with their former counterparts and ask for information and advice. Indeed, new parents should turn to their own parents for encouragement and direction.

Wise leaders study, pray, and seek sound advice in order to alleviate their anxieties and confirm their commitment to serve and lead.

After we have followed the Saviors' example, wrestled with various considerations, and received the assurance that we can succeed in our leadership position, we then must perform well and accomplish much. A leader who accepts a position without being committed to achieve appropriate goals simply blocks the path for others who want to serve and assist.

In management circles, there is a saying that goes like this: Reward or Replace! This means that when someone is not doing well in a position and does not want to learn how to do the job better, then the only alternative is to replace the person.

Since the main goal of an organization is to move forward and get the work done, having a committed leader and followers is absolutely essential for any kind of success.

In a church setting, if a home teacher or a visiting teacher, for example, is not making regular visits to a family or if those visits are perfunctory and do not attend to the real needs of the family, then that home teacher or visiting teacher may block the path for someone else to better serve the family.

All leadership positions, whether in the family, church, or workplace, give us opportunities for personal growth and development as well as provide us with more ways to render service. Leadership opportunities also allow us to discover how the organization functions. And the rewards for committed leadership invariably multiply, whether we want them to or not.

A recent graduate of a university in New York took a job with one of America's largest banking corporations. She was asked to take responsibility for writing executive memos and preparing articles for the employee's magazine.

The student quickly learned about the banking business and the organizational structure of this huge banking conglomerate by conducting interviews to get information for the articles and memos.

She also decided that even though she wasn't in the most enviable job, she would do her very best. Her efforts soon became recognized. She won recognitions for producing the best in-house publication for banking employees.

During her first year, she learned that customer service was the driving force of the banking industry. She set a marvelous example of quality work for her co-workers. When her supervisor became aware of her intense loyalty and commitment to the company, she was promoted into a position of greater responsibility.

You can tell when you are truly committed to the organizational mission, vision, and your leadership opportunity when you enlarge upon your particular assignment or calling and magnify your efforts. At your place of employment you sense a greater purpose in your daily work activities. At home and church you seek out ways to achieve exciting goals and improve people's lives. Demonstrating your commitment brings greater satisfaction to you and a stronger influence in those you are attempting to lead.

Implementing your leadership responsibilities requires you to persist under adverse circumstances. Irving Shapiro, former chairman of the board of DuPont, observed, "any fool can do it [persist] when things are going well. But how do you stay with it and keep things right when you're really in trouble? I've seen fellows who look like the greatest guys in the world and yet, when the crunch comes, they fold."

If you ever dream of doing anything great as a leader, you must consciously decide to commit to doing more than engaging in the routine necessities of leading and managing others. Following the Man called Jesus and magnifying and enlarging your various callings is a good start. When others see that you are intensely loyal and committed to your organization, whether Church, work, or family organization, and to the success of all those with whom you labor, you will be an extremely powerful, positive force and influence in their lives.

Leading with Compassion

Jesus' boldness and directness in leading people to a more meaningful way of living were always tempered by his genuine concern for their feelings and needs.

An effective leader must show an authentic concern and love for those over whom she or he has some influence. If we try to model our leadership approach after the way Jesus led his followers then section 121 of the Doctrine and Covenants must become our guide: "No power or influence can or ought to be maintained by virtue of the priesthood, only by persuasion, by long-suffering, by gentleness and meekness, and by love unfeigned; by kindness, and pure knowledge, which shall greatly enlarge the soul without hypocrisy, and without guile."

When the scribes and Pharisees brought an adulterous woman to Jesus, they confidently declared that the Law of Moses required that such a woman be stoned.

"What sayest thou," they taunted.

Jesus showed his compassion first, by ridding the woman of her accusers by saying to them, "He that is without sin among you, let him first cast a stone at her." Then, he lovingly advised the woman, "Neither do I condemn thee: go, and sin no more" (John 8:7–11).

In the case of the adulterous woman, Jesus knew that the woman was aware of what she had done, realized the condemnation and potential punishment of her act, and understood the need to change her ways.

The brevity of his response is priceless: "Neither do I condemn thee: go, and sin no more."

The whole incident suggests that we first put our own lives in order and then learn to deal more compassionately with others.

Jesus not only startled these "better than thou," pious, would be stone-throwers by asking them to look inside themselves, but he demonstrated how to be compassionate and understanding of someone who had stumbled and erred along the way.

We all make mistakes; thus it is easy to be critical and judgmental of each other. Two professional basketball officials were sitting in a hot steam room discussing their different approaches to refereeing. One gentleman was a little older than the other. Apparently, the younger official had been to a number of refresher seminars and was becoming acquainted with new rule changes and interpretations.

During the discussion, questions were raised about when contact fouls should be called, when moving screens should be penalized, and when a variety of other rule violations should be recognized. The younger referee seemed to be well informed about an infinite number of rules and regulations, and was overly anxious to display his knowledge.

The gray-haired, older referee then said something that quite surprised his younger colleague: "If I called a rule infraction every time I was aware of one, I would be stopping the game every three to five seconds! The goal of refereeing is having a fair game, not calling fouls."

Most of our mistakes are so trivial that they are not worth dwelling on. Those mistakes that are significant should be handled with great love and dispatched as quickly as possible.

All of us, husbands, wives, children, co-workers, neighbors, church members, need to be valued and feel significant. You fail to show compassion when you use tactless and offensive ways of saying things that diminish others importance. Compassion is violated through the use of verbal abuse—inappropriate and non-considered ways of saying things. Of the traditional kinds of abuse, physical, emotional, verbal, and sexual, verbal abuse is the most subtle of all. We sometimes abuse the very people we love the most, and don't even know we did it until we see the hurt in their countenance.

Verbal abuse must be guarded against every hour of the day if you want to be an energizing leader and truly lead with compassion.

Someone has said that our mouths get us into more trouble than any other part of us. Proverbs advises, "Whoso keepeth his mouth and his tongue keepeth his soul from troubles" (Proverbs 21:23).

In Psalms, David pleads with the Lord to "Set a watch, O Lord, before my mouth; keep the door of my lips" (Psalms 141:3).

James gives us some excellent advice about communicating with each other: "Let every man be swift to hear, slow to speak, and slow to wrath" (James 1:19).

A few verses following James' admonition to listen first, speak second, and control our emotions, he says, "If any man among you seem to be religious, and bridleth not his tongue, but deceiveth in his own heart, this man's religion is in vain" (James 1:26).

Often, when we are tired or in a hurry, things are spoken that threatens and undermines our relationships with others. For example, a church member was asked to offer the opening prayer at a large gathering. The person conducting the meeting approached the brother to remind him of the request and to invite him to be seated on the stand. He snappingly blurted out, "You're giving the opening prayer. Keep it brief. Take your seat." After which he quickly turned and walked away.

The curtness of the directions and the coldness of the vocal expression created a lack of feeling for the occasion. In addition, the sudden detachment and abrupt departure undermined a potentially warm and positive relationship between the person conducting and the person asked to give the prayer.

Compassionate leaders should be concerned not only with the ways in which they communicate, but also with the personal and physical needs of their followers. Jesus repeatedly demonstrated his great understanding and concern for the basic needs of his people.

Mark records that on more than one occasion Jesus called his disciples to him and explained, "I have compassion on the multitude, because they have now been with me three days and have nothing to eat: And if I send them away fasting to their own houses, they will faint by the way" (Mark 8:2–3). At that time, the people really needed food to eat, and the Savior provided that food.

Adequate food, clothing, shelter, transportation, or health care are sometimes the unexpressed but real needs of our friends and co-workers. In one situation, a personal relationship may have gone awry and greatly affected the ability of a follower to perform his or her work. For another, not having an appropriate place to work, or not having the resources to do an assignment, may be major deterrents to excellent performance.

A single parent in a ward, who had finally adjusted to life without a husband, needed something more than friendly advice and encouragement. Her car wasn't operating properly, the water taps in her apartment were leaking, the oven needed electrical work to stabilize the cooking temperature, and the children's bikes were broken.

Fortunately, a home teacher and an elder's quorum president were creative and sensitive enough to recognize some practical needs of this struggling young mother. They took steps to fix the car, replace faucet washers, repair the oven, and arrange for a couple of used bicycles to be given to the children.

Leading with compassion requires a great understanding of the needs of followers as well as a strong commitment to helping and healing wherever possible.

Jesus' personal influence and power with his followers came from his deep, sympathetic understanding of their needs, and his constant and patient efforts to respond appropriately.

You can be more compassionate by speaking kindly to people, by indicating that you value them as individuals, and by being supportive during times of need. Can you begin to realize what a great positive force you can be in others lives if you are truly committed to achieving worthwhile goals and helping others overcome problems and obstacles that may be keeping them from being fired up and moving forward in their lives? And how that positive force can be enlarged even more by attending to people's real needs, speaking kindly to them, and always preserving the confidence that people have in their own abilities and strengths?

Another way to energize people and create a positive force in them is to always be encouraging, never negative and critical, but always inspiring others with courage and confidence.

Leading with Encouragement

The simplest way to encourage others is to recognize their talents and potentials. Another way to encourage those over whom we have some influence is to follow the advice of Martin Seligman, professor, researcher, and author of *Learned Optimism*. Seligman suggests that one of most effective ways to encourage others is to use expressions of optimism.

Notice the language of Jesus as he pleads with us to believe in ourselves. He urges all people to live up to their own potential: "Ye are the salt of the earth" and "the light of the world. Let your light so shine before men, that they may see your good works, and glorify your Father which is in Heaven" (Matthew 5:13, 16).

He outlined our greatest possibilities and potentials in his simple declaration: "Be ye therefore perfect, even as your Father which is in heaven is perfect" (Matthew 5:48). We can lead in the same manner, giving encouragement and lifting our associates with words and actions that suggest they have unlimited potential.

A famous university football coach, with one of the best winning records, does everything in his power to get his football players to believe in themselves. He teaches them the fundamentals of the game: blocking, tackling, and team work. Then he encourages each player to perform to the best of his ability. He does not dwell on their faults or their weaknesses, but focuses on their strengths.

This coach uses a barrage of positive comments to energize his players to perform at their highest levels: "You can do it, son." "They can't knock you down." "You're the best."

Each year the team's objective is to play in a major bowl game. In practice, players see how committed the coach is to achieving the goal and how totally committed he is to them. They in turn respond by doing things on the playing field that other coaches say border on the supernatural. Accordingly, they receive an invitation, each year, to play in a college bowl game.

Ken Melrose, chairman and CEO of the Toro Company, articulates the importance of this view when he asserts, "you have it within your power to help your company develop a new culture—with a climate of trust defined by a set of values that stresses the dignity and importance of every employee. This is the service you can best offer your company as a leader."

A sage once said, "The best way to change people is to treat them as if they had already changed." In other words, respecting a person's talents and potential encourages positive change.

When the pathway to a better way of life became rough and difficult for Jesus' followers, he lifted their heads and hearts by substituting understanding for fear and cheerfulness for a sad countenance. "Be of good cheer" became one of Christ's more familiar phrases.

In healing a palsy stricken man, Jesus encouraged him to "be of good cheer; thy sins be forgiven thee" (Matthew 9:2). Nearer the end of his life, Jesus explained to his disciples that they would be scattered, "every man to his own," and that they would be sorrowful because he must leave them. However, Jesus reminded them to "be of good cheer: I have overcome the world" (John 16:33).

During Paul the Apostle's day, Paul was going from city to city trying to preach the gospel. His life was being threatened, and he faced all kinds of tribulations. After one particularly difficult day, the scriptures witness: "And the night following the Lord stood by him, and said, Be of good cheer, Paul: For as thou hast testified of me in Jerusalem, so must thou bear witness also at Rome" (Acts 23:11).

We can smile a little as we imagine the Lord saying to us, "Be of good cheer. I know that you got beat up a little today. But wait until you see what's in store for you over there in Rome tomorrow!"

On the other hand, we can also comprehend the encouragement that comes from someone, whom we admire, filled with enlightenment, peace, and power, who visits us when we are sick and discouraged and says, "Be of good cheer. It is I, your neighbor. Do not be afraid. I can help."

If we are true followers of Christ, we can go to our families, friends, and work associates with the same encouraging influence. We can say, with great love and confidence, "Don't worry. I am here. Everything is going to be alright now."

Happiness is not an external condition; it is an attitude and state of mind. Though you may be influenced by conditions and events which surround you, you have final control over whether you are happy or sad. Many researchers in the area of human psychology now believe that "discouragement is a decision that we make." We get to decide whether we will be happy and optimistic about life or whether we will wallow around in sadness, self pity, and discouragement.

Sometimes we forget that Jesus and his apostles faced dreary, rainy winter days in Jerusalem. The weather was not always sunny and pleasant. They also had to deal with unscrupulous officials in the local government and crafty spokesmen of various religious groups. Life was not easy.

Had Jesus based his happiness on others or the weather, he would have been riding an emotional roller coaster for most of his life. Because happiness is an attitude, we can greatly influence our state of being.

A university professor was sitting in his office with a big grin on his face. A colleague of his walked past the open door, noticed the large smile, and inquired, "What's wrong?"

"Nothing," replied the still grinning professor. The inquirer then commented on all the problems the department was facing and explained that these were difficult times and many people were unhappy.

"How can you be smiling at a time like this?" his colleague asked.

The reply was utterly simple and startling. ""I choose to be happy."

The professor was not ignorant to the inequities and administrative problems around him, and he was trying to correct some obvious wrongs. However, he refused to let his happiness constantly fluctuate because of someone else's unhappiness or sad circumstances.

Jesus encouraged his followers to be of good cheer. He constantly tried to gladden their hearts and raise their spirits. In the Sermon on the Mount, for example, Christ tried specifically to explain nine Beatitudes or ways to receive comfort and continuing happiness.

Each Beatitude begins with the word "Blessed." To be "blessed" means to be happy, fortunate, and content. If we want constant, inner happiness, we can choose to live these spiritual rules for happiness. Jesus himself shared happiness because he had inner contentment—he lived the Beatitudes before teaching them.

To follow the example of Jesus is to go directly against the advice that the world usually recommends for happiness.

The world condemns the external acts of killing, adultery, and oath swearing. However, Jesus condemned the very thought itself. In our popular vernacular you can almost hear Jesus saying, "Don't even think about it!" Most acts that undermine our own and others happiness begin with an inappropriate thought. If an impure thought enters our mind, as Elder Boyd K. Packer says, "don't let it build a nest on your head, get rid of it as quickly as possible." Control the thought and you control the act (Matthew 5 and 6).

The whole Sermon on the Mount is an attempt by Jesus to help us look inwardly. By actively examining our own thoughts and attitudes, we exercise control over how we feel.

Another wonderful way to encourage others and develop a positive force in their lives is to help them see the rewards that accrue as the result of the successful accomplishment of a task. People are frequently encouraged and energized by visualizing the contribution, money, or opportunities that are associated with the completion of a goal. People trying to get out of debt visualize the debt-free life. People who try to complete classes in an educational institution focus on the beneficial outcomes of a degree or certificate of completion to provide energy to keep going.

Often, people who are contributing regularly to a savings and investment program are highly involved because they visualize the good life of retirement without financial worry. As a leader at work or in your family, you too can encourage and motivate others by helping your work associates and children see the benefits that will accrue both intrinsically and extrinsically if they complete the task or achieve the goal that you or they have articulated.

If you choose to be an encouraging leader and be happy during the day and replace discouragement and gloom with hope and joy, you must begin to free our own heart. At the same time you need to encourage others to do the same.

Like the Savior, you should lie down at night knowing that you tried your best not to offend or discourage anyone. Your conscience is clear and your sleep is restful and rejuvenating.

Everyone Can Lead

All of us, men and women alike, though riddled with human imperfections and limitations, can succeed in leadership opportunities by seeking the same attributes of commitment, compassion, and cheerfulness that characterized Christ's remarkable leadership style.

Jesus recognized the weaknesses and frailties of the original twelve apostles, but saw beyond them to greater strengths and leadership potentials: Peter had an impulsive nature, but he grew in stature to become the head of the church in those days. Matthew was a hated publican, but he wrote a sympathetic account of Jesus' life that has influenced the lives of millions. John was called the son of thunder because of his outrageous temper, but today he is universally know as "John, the beloved."

Every one of us has the potential to become a more effective leader by creating a positive force that inspires those over whom we have some responsibility.

Jesus was fully committed to his work, consummately compassionate toward people, and consistently encouraging in the face of adversity.

The Savior's invitation is extended to each of us: "Follow me and become even as I am."

3

The Third Key:
Invite Others to Follow

One day, after Jesus returned to his home town of Nazareth, Luke recorded, "He went into the synagogue on the sabbath day, and stood up for to read" (Luke 4:16).

Picture Jesus entering the synagogue to read from the scriptures. From the Book of Esaias, he reads the phrase, "The Spirit of the Lord is upon me, because he hath anointed me to preach the gospel to the poor" and closes the book. He then sits down, the eyes of the entire congregation on him. He adds, "This day is this scripture fulfilled in your ears" (Luke 4:17–21).

The gripping events that often engulf a bold and courageous leader followed: They seized him, dragged him to the outskirts of the city, to the brow of a hill, to throw him headfirst over the cliff. However, the dramatic concluding act was not to occur as they expected: "But he passing through the midst of them went his way" (Luke 4:30).

Unfazed by the ire of the unruly crowd, Jesus took command of the situation and calmly walked through the mob in complete control. Jesus did not hesitate to take the lead and invite people to follow him. Here is a person with powerful leadership abilities; a person with purpose, direction and goals. This is a "Come, Follow Me" (Luke 18:22).

The simplest of phrases often convey the most intriguing and powerful meanings to the human mind. Such is the case with the utterance

"Come, Follow Me." The essence of leadership is expressed in these words.

To lead is to go before or show the way; guide the direction, course, action, or opinion. To lead is often thought of as being out in front, or proceeding first.

The phrase, "Come, follow me," perfectly characterizes the primary act of leadership. The leader goes before and requests others to follow. Jesus did not wait for others—he led the way.

Although this may seem elementary, the life of Jesus constantly demonstrates that he took the first step and invited others to follow. The scriptures are filled with incidents in which Jesus led the way.

A simple instance occurred eight days after feeding five thousand with five loaves and two fishes. Luke records, "He took Peter and John and James, and went up into a mountain to pray" (Luke 9:28). He did not say, "Go up there. I'll meet you later." Christ led the way and then he asked the disciples to follow him.

Leadership, as demonstrated by Jesus, consists of taking the initiative, being out in front, and firmly but patiently pleading with others to come and follow.

Consider the feast of the dedication in Jerusalem. It was winter and Jesus was walking in the temple in Solomon's porch.

The Jews were divided over whether Jesus was a devil, mad, or the Christ. A number of the Jews gathered around Jesus and asked, "How long dost thou make us to doubt? If thou be the Christ, tell us plainly." Jesus replied, "I told you, and ye believed not."

Once again Jesus seized the initiative and led the way. He explained that he was the Good Shepherd. "My sheep know my voice," he said. ""If you don't believe me, then believe in my good works. I do them in the name of My Father. They bear witness of me. The Father and I are one. I am the Son of God. Believe in me. Follow me!" (See John 10).

Filled with resentment and rage, the Jews wanted to stone him. Jesus did not flinch. Buoyed up by knowing who he was and his purpose in life, his being was flooded with calmness and strength. Not a rock was thrown nor a hand laid upon him as he departed out of their presence.

Leading, as the Jesus did, has four requisites associated with it. These preconditions seem impellingly appropriate to examine now.

1. Visionary Purpose

Among the leadership characteristics of the eminently successful Jesus, one of the clearest is that he was driven forward by the vision of his earthly purpose. Even as a youth, he understood his great and wonderful calling. The incident in the temple, where his parents found him "sitting in the midst of doctors, both hearing them, and asking them questions," illustrates this deep understanding.

His reply to the anxious question of his Mother "How is it that ye sought me? wist ye not that I must be about my Father's business?" clearly indicates the vision of his purpose (Luke 3:49).

As a leader, you must also know what business you are about. You must have personal goals and a direction. This is illustrated by a statement of goals appearing in a term paper written by a university student, who was also the owner and manager of a small business:

> I desire with all my heart, with all the fiber of my being, and in deep humility, to be able to emulate the life of Jesus Christ, for he is indeed the perfect example of an effective leader. I intend to be industrious, compassionate, and encouraging in my endeavors to be a successful businessman, father, and husband. Specifically, I hope to be a good listener, to create a vision, to involve others, and to show an unconditional love to those with whom I come in contact. The values I presently hold dear will be supported and remain consistent as I display my commitment to these principles in daily example to my family and associates.

You should clarify and develop your own set of goals. Setting personal goals makes you a more attractive leader. Unless those around you see you striving for worthy achievements, they will not look to you as a good example to follow. They will quickly recognize that you are not committed to the tasks that need to be accomplished.

Leaders in organizations have the opportunity and obligation to envision future expectations of the organization. Almost all scholars agree upon this one point. Leaders that have made a difference in major corporations around the world were visionary; they dared to dream dreams. They imagined in their minds what could be, and invited others to follow by articulating the dream in a way that made it possible to achieve.

Researchers and practitioners commonly agree that people look for something beyond the wages and benefits of a job to excite and motivate them. Employees desire to be part of something bigger. They want to share in a group or organizational goal.

Employees at a large aircraft facility recently spoke about *their* company and how *they* had just sent a missile into orbit. It sounded as if they owned the company and had personally fired the missile from the launch pad that was located over 2000 miles from where they worked. They were excited because they were part of a big and wonderful accomplishment.

A leader foresees the end of a project and formulates ideas for possible outcomes. The question for the leader is "What do we want to have happen?" The answer to such a question is nearly always found in an image of the end result, in a vision of the future.

Consider any project or organization—a company party, a business organization, or your family.. What is the most critical asset that you as leader can have? The answer is a vision of what the party, business, or family could be like.

Effective leaders imagine the great view of the very best. What should happen at the very best party? What should occur in the very best business or the very best family? Likewise, what expectations should be set for the very best family, or very best business organization?

A newly organized ward Relief Society presidency held their first leadership meeting. The new president, a young, wise woman, proceeded to describe her expectations and dreams for the Relief Society to her counselors and secretary. She desired, more than anything, to have the sisters unite in a spirit of charity and love for each other. She also wanted them to be fortified and inspired to give service to their families and neighbors.

This Relief Society president felt that her counselors, who were going to be key people in leading the sisters, should have an opportunity to add to the vision. She then turned to her counselors and asked them to dream about what a perfect union of women would look like and feel like.

Each, in turn, contributed greatly to what an ideal Relief Society should be like. The first counselor said that "all should share the experience of coming together to receive enlightened instruction. Those who were not present should be immediately contacted and the information shared with them so that they would feel included and informed."

"I see our sisters in constant contact with each other, strengthening and supporting each other outside of our regular meetings. They network together for increased motivation, additional help, and rendering compassionate service to each other," said the other counselor.

Thus was born a vision for this particular Relief Society. A vision may not be 100 percent practical or 100 percent achievable, but it must be exciting and stimulating. It must stir our imagination and cause us to reach higher.

A mother and father can dream together about their own family: What should it be like? How should members act? What directions should it take?

Bishops can create in their minds and with the help of their counselors the ideal ward. Young women leaders can find in their minds and hearts the best application of the Young Women's program for their girls. A deacon's quorum president, with the help of an advisor, can envision the very best quorum meetings and projects.

Years ago, the vision of being a great stake was grasped by a young stake president in a rural, outlying area of the Church. When the Church published a list of the leading Stakes, he studied the names of the stakes as he milked the cows on his farm. He wondered why certain stakes were listed. He met with the high council and asked them what it would take to be listed as the number one Stake in the Church.

The stake clerks reviewed the requirements and gathered figures that showed the difference between his stake and the Number One Stake. He began to get a vision of where the stake should be going and what it should be doing. Then, at the next stake conference, he vividly described his vision to the stake membership and counseled them to "follow the stake leaders."

The bishops, priesthood quorum leaders, Mutual presidencies, Sunday school presidencies, Relief Society presidencies, and the general membership caught the vision. They all agreed to do what was necessary to make this stake the number one Stake in the Church for the very next year.

Attendance at meetings shot up, and ward activities increased.

Priesthood quorums involved their members in every way possible within the stake boundaries of the rural communities. Sunday School teachers, home teachers, visiting teachers, and Aaronic priesthood and young women leaders held exciting classes and implemented powerful member activation programs.

At the end of the year, when the final reports were submitted, excitement and anticipation flamed through the stake. When the next list of outstanding stakes was published, heading the list was the stake in the mountains of Utah—Stake Number One. The vision was fulfilled.

Outstanding leaders have lofty expectations and visions of great achievements that involve all members of the organization. Effective leaders have a clear and precise image or picture of what the organization or activity could be like. Leaders must also understand the potential of their followers to contribute successfully to achieving the envisioned goals.

As president of the Church of Jesus Christ of Latter-day Saints, Ezra Taft Benson saw the world flooded with copies of the Book of Mormon. That vision stirred the imagination of millions of faithful followers. President Benson knew of their potential to accomplish such a magnificent mission. The response from Church members was phenomenal. Every family and organization in the Church contributed copies of the Book of Mormon to be distributed all over the world by missionaries and local Church leaders. The enactment of the vision has clearly contributed to the world at large, and benefited the growth and development of participating families and Church members.

Similarly, a Mormon temple presidency reported to President Spencer W. Kimball that they were the number-one temple in the Church in terms of activities taking place within its walls. Although President Kimball expressed deep appreciation, he knew the potential of the patrons to do even more, so he encouraged the temple presidency to "lengthen their stride."

A few years ago, a little church branch in a southern community had an experienced leader who was trying to implement all the policies and procedures found in the handbook. Needless to say, the vision was great, but implementation became a near disaster because of inexperienced followers—clearly a case of the leader getting too involved in the procedures without a realistic vision of the followers' strengths and weaknesses.

By keeping the vision bright and adjusting to the ability of members, the dream of achieving an excellent Church branch quickly moved forward. In a few years the branch became a fully staffed ward, meeting in a small beautiful chapel.

Robert D. Haas, as chairman and chief executive officer of Levi Strauss & Company, has overseen revolutionary changes in the way his company designs, manufactures, markets, and sells clothing. Haas enjoys talking about his leadership approach and is quick to point out that "at our company, we recognize we have 36,000 pairs of eyes and ears that are in the marketplace all the time. We really want to involve as many people as possible in shaping the future."

A stimulating vision of the future can bind people together as a group. An inspiring and worthy vision can unite hundreds of people and move them forward with considerable energy even though they may face almost insurmountable difficulties.

Great causes produce great effort. The Revolutionary War had "a free country" as its vision. Martin Luther King had a "dream." Political campaigns couched in images like "A thousand points of light" and "A bridge into the next century" seem to provide a vision of the future and a condition better that what we are in at the present time.

When the causes are really great and powerfully described, people are willing to give their lives to achieve the victory. We don't need anyone to give their lives for an organizational cause or vision, but we do need people who willingly give more effort and thought to making things better at work, home, Church, and in the community.

Visions and missions need to sound lofty and idealistic or they are not very energizing to anyone. Read this vision from McDonald's: "To satisfy the world's appetite for good food, well-served, at a price people can afford." Get the picture?

The world's appetite is part of their dream. Every McDonald's employee is asked to think about how to satisfy the world's appetite, serve food that is hot and fresh, in the most comfortable environment, and do everything at a price that people can afford.

Remember the conclusion of William Faulkner's brilliant acceptance speech when he received the Nobel Prize in literature. In brief, he said, "Man will not only endure but triumph!" We were not created to endure work but to find joy in working and creating something better than it was when we arrived.

Visions and missions that challenge the status quo and provoke us to think greater thoughts need to be developed and shared at every level of every organization and in our families. Top level managers, Church leaders, and parents usually develop attractive visions, missions and goals. Various units in the organization then contribute to those goals and visions with their input. Individuals in every kind of organization should be allowed and encouraged to give their insight on what and how things can be achieved.

Leaders recognize that they and their associates have both strengths and weaknesses. Everyone has various gifts and talents. All have God-like potential. Leaders shape a vision of the future that capitalizes on what everyone brings to the situation. They also keep in mind what is best for the people in the organization.

Jesus' example of leadership is positive, encouraging, and challenging. His vision included the idea that each follower has a yearning to succeed, and if required will accomplish the extraordinary. As leaders you should have the same expectations of your followers.

Leaders with a visionary purpose light the way so that others may see and follow. As with Jesus, you too should be able to say, "Come and follow me."

2. Constant Direction

Followers need dreams and visions to stir their imaginations and excite their souls. However, they also need to understand *how* to achieve the vision. They need to have specific, achievable, and practical goals to motivate them toward the larger vision and greater mission.

Jesus introduced a grand objective to his followers: "Be ye, therefore, perfect, even as your Father which is in heaven is perfect" (Matthew 5:48). This was the dream. Do not just be a good person, or only think about becoming a great teacher. Imagine becoming as perfect as Father in Heaven.

Jesus urged, prodded, and invited his followers to steer consistently and persistently in a straight, narrow course that leads in one direction: toward perfection.

Jesus admonished his followers to avoid distractions and avoid getting lost along the way by keeping in the center of the path. He also gave some very specific suggestions about what a person should do to move toward perfection. He said that:

Whosoever shall smite thee on thy right cheek, turn to him the other also. And if any man will sue thee at the law, and take away thy coat, let him have thy cloak also. And whosoever shall compel thee to go a mile, go with him twain. Give to him that asketh thee, and from him that would borrow of thee turn not thou away. Ye have heard that it hath been said, Thou shalt love thy neighbor, and hate thine enemy. But I say unto you, Love your enemies, bless them that curse you, do good to them that hate you, and pray for them which despitefully use you, and persecute you. (Matthew 5:39–44)

The vision is perfection; the goal is to love your enemies. Jesus explained how to accomplish the goal: turn your other cheek when struck, walk two miles when compelled to walk one, and so forth.

A great leader needs a bright vision of what the organization and its members ought to be like, and a clear idea of what is to be accomplished in order to achieve the vision. We call this our desired direction. Sometimes it is called a mission statement.

The mission of Bonneville International Corporation, the Church's communications company, is to provide personal growth opportunities for employees, to enhance the effectiveness, power, influence, and value of properties, and to exert positive leadership in the broadcast industry (*BYU Today*, November 1989, 34). These statements represent the vision translated into a direction. They indicate what the organization is committed to do to bring about the vision.

A mission statement encapsulates and epitomizes the unique reason for the existence of the organization. The priesthood quorums of the Church, for example, may derive their missions from two basic values: (1) Every individual is of immense worth, and (2) each family in the Church is a government within itself (*Melchizedek Priesthood Personal Study Guide 1989*, 1988, 1). That is, a priesthood quorum creates its mission or basic purpose from these two assumptions.

The mission unifies the organization and provides it with a sense of direction and rationale for its existence. As a leader, you must set a course that is constant and clear in the minds of those with whom you work. The direction should not be mediocre and imprecise. The direction should be toward perfection.

Once the vision is established, the direction you must go, and the things you need to do must be understood by all members of your organization in order to turn the vision into a reality. After we envision the ideal Relief Society, priesthood quorum, family, or work team, we need to ask ourselves, "What do we need to accomplish to achieve the grand objective?"

A father and mother, concerned with negative influences outside the home, wanted to build a unified family. They imagined members of the family loving, supporting, and sustaining each other. Their vision was clear. How to achieve their goal required more than hope that the family would become close and strong.

This father and mother found it rather easy to love each other and be as one, because they were accustomed to talking frequently with each other. When a problem arose, however, they had to take time to counsel together and find a solution. Consequently, these parents decided that the whole family could benefit by talking frequently to each other and counseling together when concerns arose.

After some deliberation, the family agreed to hold a council to decide on some ways to develop a closer family. It didn't take long for the younger members of the family to see the benefits of meeting together. They were able to help make important decisions, share their goals and dreams for the future, and seek the support and help of other family members to make their own difficulties and burden a little lighter.

The first goal agreed upon was to hold regular family meetings. The second goal was to offer helpful suggestions and service to members of the family who were having a little difficulty in school. The third goal was to seek personal inspiration each day for direction and strength.

Other achievable goals were identified and plans were set. The vision of a happy, unified family was vividly described so that the children could not only participate in the weekly meetings and achievements, but also feel part of something bigger and greater than themselves—an eternal, celestial family whose unity and love continues forever and ever.

Do not be discouraged if all of your goals are not immediately achieved. Accomplishing some of the goals is exciting, and a sign that you have made a good start. We all like to feel that we are making progress. Little successes breed confidence and enthusiasm.

To be associated with a business organization that is making a profit and expanding its operations is an exciting feeling. No business, educational institution, or family is yet perfect. Each can have a great vision of achievable goals, and directions that give the members confidence in the future.

3. Speak with Conviction

Jesus used every opportunity to speak enthusiastically and passionately about his goals and aspirations. Matthew recounts how Jesus commanded the Apostles to conduct their business:

> Go not into the way of the Gentiles and into any city
> of the Samaritans enter ye not: But go rather to the
> lost sheep of the house of Israel. (Matthew 10:5–42)

You can feel the intensity of his explanations as he directed them to "preach, saying the kingdom of heaven is at hand." Listen carefully as Jesus urges them to be selective: "And whosoever shall not receive you, nor hear your words, when ye depart out of that house or city, shake off the dust of your feet." These words were not spoken casually, but uttered with conviction.

Corporate business leaders and great political leaders seize every opportunity to articulate their views over and over again to individuals and groups who will listen.

Many leaders forget that it is as necessary to communicate the vision as it is to create the vision. A good idea doesn't run around by itself and find lodging in the hearts of people. A dream and its accompanying goals must be told and retold in every possible way.

A new corporate president was successful with one of America's largest carmakers because he used his personality and various media to convey the mission of his company to employees and the public at large. His dreams and hopes captivated the imagination of thousands of people. Subsequently, he was able to move this large company from a deficit financial position to a financially successful one.

How did the multitudes react to Christ as they listened to the Sermon on the Mount? As we read in Matthew, "And it came to pass, when Jesus had ended these sayings, the people were astonished at his doctrine: For he taught them as one having authority, and not as the scribes" (Matthew 7:28–29).

In like manner, President Harold B. Lee inspired members of the Church throughout the world when he explained that conference talks were the "mind and will of the Lord." He exhorted everyone to make these messages their "walk and talk" for the next six months.

Those conference addresses were read and studied in priesthood quorum meetings, family gatherings, Relief Society meetings and sacrament meetings. Home teachers articulated the messages and the spirit of conference to their families. Seminary and institute of religion classes studied and discussed the conference addresses.

We can only conclude that powerful leadership involves speaking and communicating with conviction. Deep and abiding conviction comes from speaking with the Spirit.

Speak with the Spirit

Jesus explained that when you speak with the spirit, you will have the confidence to face difficult situations and speak with authority and conviction (See Matthew 10:19–28). We can obtain confirmation from the Spirit concerning what to say and how to say it.

Jesus exhorted us in these words:

> You are the light of the world. A city that is set on a hill cannot be hid. Neither do men light a candle and put it under a bushel, but on a candlestick; and it giveth light unto all that are in the house. Let your light so shine before men, that they may see your good works, and glorify your Father which is in heaven. (Matthew 5:14–16)

Jesus prompted us to take our great ideas and commitments out of our own minds and hearts, and speak up and share those views with others. Elder Russell M. Nelson of the Quorum of the Twelve describes what it is like when we draw upon the spirit:

> Friday evening before the Solemn Assembly, to be attended by all the priesthood leaders of fourteen stakes the following morning, I was on an airplane with Sister Nelson and with President Hinckley. I leaned over to him seated right in front of me and I said, "President, I'd be pleased to receive whatever instructions you'd care to give me about the subject

matter, length of time. Whatever direction you would like to give me—I'd be most grateful for it." "Please!" he said, "talk as long as you want on any subject you want. You're the servant of the Lord. You give the message the Lord wants you to give."

We got to St. George to the motel about ten o'clock at night. I kissed my sweetheart goodnight, tucked her in, and then prayed. I don't think I went to bed that night. I sat up in that room pouring over the scriptures, studying, searching, and writing. It came, and the following morning President Hinckley called on me to be the first speaker. I gave the message that came between midnight and 5:00 A.M. (*Melchizedek Priesthood Personal Study Guide 1989*, 196–97)

Like Jesus, we too have many occasions to speak with conviction, and to receive the same kind of reaction that the Savior did: "for all the people were very attentive to hear him" (Luke 19:48).

The conviction and dynamism with which Christ spoke also came from a deep-seated understanding of his divine heritage. As mortals with knowledge of our divine roots, we can also speak with calm and dynamic insight. As leaders we have both the charge and opportunity to follow the example of the Savior and speak out in support of good causes.

Be Prepared to Answer Questions

Not only must dynamic leaders speak with conviction, but they must also be prepared to respond to questions raised by followers. Jesus, through confidence and calmness, conviction and understanding, changed difficult situations into moments of direction and focus.

When performing miracles, Jesus was regularly challenged to justify his acts. Mark recounts the healing of a man with a withered hand. The Pharisees watched to see whether Jesus would heal the man. Their purpose was to accuse him of violating the Sabbath (Mark 3:1–6).

In a thinly veiled dialogue, the Pharisees challenged him with the question "Is it lawful to heal on the sabbath days?"

His reply was neither condescending nor argumentative, but direct and gentle: "Is it lawful," he asked, "to do good on the sabbath days?"

He broadened the issue by asking if it was lawful to do evil, to save life, or to kill? Facing a restless group of learned antagonists, Jesus drove his point home with a provocative question-parable.

He asked, "What man shall there be among you, that shall have one sheep, and if it fall into a pit on the sabbath day, will he not lay hold on it, and lift it out?"

Then, Jesus offered the powerful conclusion in simplicity but with conviction: "How much then is a man better than a sheep?"

What did Jesus do then? Did he play to the crowd? Did he seek to avenge their accusations? Did he chortle with his disciples? No, he quietly called upon the injured man and asked him to stretch forth his hand. Then he restored him to health. The issue was settled.

Another example, showing how Jesus was prepared to answer questions, occurred when on the sabbath he healed a woman who had been infirm for eighteen years. The ruler of the synagogue responded indignantly to the healing. Jesus answered with a firm and direct response:

> Thou hypocrite, doth not each one of you on the sabbath loose his ox or his ass from the stall, and lead him away to watering? And ought not this woman . . . be loosed from this bond on the sabbath day? (Luke 13:10–16)

Rather than argue with the ruler, Christ skillfully drew out a relevant answer with a carefully placed question. The challenge offered by the ruler was firmly diverted and captured as a strong reason for Jesus' actions.

To be effective leaders in the home, parents must listen to the questions of children and respond to them with appropriate answers. Failing to give a response, or responding ambiguously, causes confusion and misunderstanding.

During a family gathering, the children unanimously agreed that they would like to take a vacation to New England. They had been impressed at school with the historical significance of the events that had transpired in the founding of America in the New England area.

When they queried their parents about the possibility of such a trip, they met an awkward silence and some incoherent comments about the costs of such a vacation.

The alert, optimistic smiles of the little children quickly vanished, to be replaced by expressions of hurt and bewilderment. Later, they asked questions about whether Dad was seriously ill or Mom was expecting a baby. Why else would they not be encouraged to pursue such a magnificent vacation? Rather than avoiding the issue, the parents should reassure the children that costs were the main problem and that they might be remedied in a variety of ways, including taking a shorter trip with the same purpose.

In any case, parents, managers, church leaders, and anyone wanting to lead and influence people must respond to questions in the clearest, kindest, and most optimistic way possible.

Jesus' approach to leadership demonstrates that people will follow when leaders express a visionary purpose, provide constant direction toward that purpose, and speak with conviction. Another characteristic of the great leader that attracts others is the use of patient instructions.

4. Patient Instruction

Jesus must have become weary of constantly explaining his divine mission and that he would die and be resurrected. His responses show that he was slightly provoked, on occasion. This was apparent when he asked his disciples questions such as, "And why call ye me, Lord, Lord, and do not the things which I say?" (Luke 6:46)

Even though he showed signs of being weary, he persisted in teaching a lesson. In this case the point was revealed by a story of the builder who built his house on a rock foundation in contrast to the person who built a house directly on the earth, and the storm beat against it and it fell in ruin (Luke 6:48–49). This shows that Jesus' great leadership and attractiveness as one to be followed involved an unerring patience in giving instructions.

The scriptures show, directly and indirectly, that Jesus " . . . went throughout the city and village, preaching and shewing the glad tidings of the kingdom of God: and the twelve were with him" (Luke 8:1).

How was he received? Luke reports that "the people gladly received him: for they were all waiting for him" (Luke 8:40).

How did he approach the task of patient instruction? As Luke states, "he taught daily in the temple" (Luke 19:47).

While teaching, he was sometimes harangued and challenged. When asked by feigning deceivers, "Is it lawful for us to give tribute unto

Caesar, or no?" Jesus answered with the well-known and classic response: "Render therefore unto Caesar the things which be Caesar's, and unto God the things which be God's" (Luke 20:25). What type of reaction did his teaching bring? "And they could not take hold of his words before the people: and they marveled at his answer, and held their peace."

Patiently instructing all attentive listeners, counseling with his disciples, and directing his Apostles, Jesus drew people to him. "And in the daytime he was teaching in the temple, and at night he went out, and abode in the mount that is called the Mount of Olives. And all the people came early in the morning to him in the temple, for to hear him" (Luke 21:37–38). "They came and came: And early in the morning, he came *again* into the temple, all the people came unto him; and he sat down, and taught them" (John 8:2 emphasis added).

An excellent example of patient instructions is personified by one of the General Authorities of the Church of Jesus Christ of Latter-day Saints, Elder Boyd K. Packer. He spends many days attending stake and regional conferences where he instructs individuals, groups, and large audiences. His aim is to illuminate the grand mission of the gospel and the Church, and give directions for achieving appropriate goals along the way.

In a stake priesthood leadership meeting, Elder Packer asked the stake president to call the meeting to order, sing, pray, and then turn the time over to him. Elder Packer then gave some brief introductory remarks and said that he would be happy to respond to any questions that those present might have.

For about an hour and a half, interesting and important questions were asked. Elder Packer listened attentively. He thoroughly and clearly answered each question to the satisfaction of the questioner.

"What is the biggest weakness of the Saints along the Wasatch Front?" "What should I do as a quorum president when some of my faithful members do not attend the temple regularly?" "What is the responsibility of the bishop when some members of the ward do not respond to the pleading of the Prophet to prepare their families for the perilous times that are rapidly approaching?"

After answering these kinds of questions, the meeting ended. Leaders congregated in the hallways and commented about the marvelous personal instructions that each one had received from a General Authority of the Church.

Jesus was untiring in his efforts to (1) create the vision that would attract his followers. (2) He was constant, never veering from the goal being pursued. (3) When he spoke he did so enthusiastically with power and conviction. Multitudes of people came to hear his message. And then with remarkable patience (4) he instructed and guided his followers to a clear understanding of how to live life more abundantly.

To be effective as leaders, we need to follow the Savior's example and learn how to create a lively vision for those whom we lead and to communicate that vision to those whom we lead.

4

The Fourth Key:
Enable Followers to Act

Jesus went out into a mountain to pray. When it was morning, he came down from the mountain and called his followers together. From them he selected twelve whom he also called apostles (see Luke 6:12–16).

The scriptures do not indicate that the newly appointed apostles immediately began their work. Even when we read in Luke that Jesus "called his twelve disciples together, and gave them power and authority," we fail to get an indication that the apostles then proceeded to engage in their work.

It is not until we read the tenth chapter of Matthew that we discover the full process that Jesus used to enable his followers to act. This same process was used again for enabling the Seventy (see Luke 10).

Nothing is so discouraging to a person than to be invited to participate in the achievement of a wonderful goal or important assignment and not have the resources or understanding of how to accomplish it successfully. So many times at home, church and work, people are invited to become involved in a task or assignment and they don't even know the expectation or standards to be achieved while accomplishing the assignment because they were never informed.

Your responsibility as a leader is to help others enjoy the sweet taste of success. If you're leading effectively, others accomplish something far greater than they had ever imagined possible. You stand by them and support them all the way. You provide them with the resources to succeed and make sure that they understand how to use those resources efficiently.

Five distinguishable stages may be identified in the enabling process:

Calling

Empowering

Instructing

Sending

Reporting

Leadership involves more than simply authorizing, commissioning, or assigning people to do things. Jesus clearly recognized that leaders must follow a process and provide understanding and resources that not only allow but also open the way for followers to take action. Notice carefully these five steps that Jesus used to enable followers to act.

The Five Steps

1. He Called Them. This first step involves calling people into assignments and positions. Jesus consciously and deliberately selected twelve individuals from the multitude of disciples and gave them the position of apostles. They were identified and given titles. Likewise, to enable those with whom you work, you must be certain that they are clearly identified and given appropriate designations. The designated calling, assignment, position, or title enables individuals to do the work. They are identified as those who have been chosen to engage in the work. Less ambiguity exists and more clarity prevails. This is an important first step in the enabling process. But, this is only the first step.

2. He Empowered Them. Even if called into or appointed or even elected to a position, few people feel comfortable about moving ahead unless they have been given the power and authority to do so. Luke records that "then he called his twelve disciples together, and gave them power and authority. . ." (Luke 9:1). The assignment of authority is usually done in a formal way, through some simple ceremony so that everyone recognizes that the person called to the position has actually been accorded the authority to act in the position. Sometimes just putting a name plate on a door serves that function, but in many organizations a formal introduction and official recognition is important.

3. He Instructed Them. Often leaders forget that, even when people have the authority to act, they must be instructed specifically on how to get started. Matthew explains that "these twelve Jesus sent forth, and commanded them . . ." (Matthew 10:5). The term "commanded" may be interpreted to mean instructed because the commands involved information about what they were to do as they went about their work. For example, the apostles were to go to "the lost sheep of the house of Israel, to provide neither gold, nor silver, nor brass in your purses, nor scrip for your journey, neither two coats, neither shoes, nor yet staves" (Matthew 10: 11–14). To be an effective leader, you too must instruct your followers in what they are to do. We sometimes think of this step as "training," or human resource development, but it is apparent that the proper instruction of followers is a major step in the process of enabling them to act.

4. He Sent Them. This is such a logical step in the process of enabling followers, but it is one that is often overlooked. It is essential for an effective leader to actually indicate that followers should proceed to act. Luke says, "And he sent them to preach the kingdom of God, and to heal the sick" (Luke 9:2). Likewise, as a leader you must also send your followers to do their work. This is, of course, a motivating send off, one that encourages and uplifts your followers. This is a SEND OFF, a salutation and a celebration. They are being sent to be successful.

5. He Had Them Report to Him. When Leaders instruct followers and send them out to do their work, they also need a way to discover how things are going. Luke explains that "And the apostles, when they were returned, told him all that they had done" (Luke 9:10). Jesus did the most efficient thing he could: he asked each apostle to report about how well he had completed the work.

When followers report back after taking action, they are often ready to discuss difficulties and problems. They may need guidance and redirection. This is done best in private rather than in public. Luke reported that Jesus did take his followers aside: "And he took them, and went aside privately" (Luke 9:10). Counseling with followers is achieved best in private because it allows for open and frank discussion prior to meeting with a larger group. Personal feelings can be protected more easily in private meetings. In fact, Mark explained that after Jesus cast out the evil spirit from the young boy, "his disciples asked him privately, Why could not we cast him out?" As a leader, you must take some opportunities to counsel privately with those who need assistance and can benefit from guidance and counsel.

Jesus taught the disciples, counseled with them, and explained marvelous things in private. On occasion, he advised them that "blessed are your eyes, for they see; and your ears, for they hear. For verily I say unto you, That many prophets and righteous men have desired to see those things which ye see, and have not seen them: and to hear those things which ye hear, and have not heard them" (Matthew 13:16–17).

These five stages—calling, empowering, instructing, sending, and reporting (CEISR)—are the essence of the process of enabling those with whom you work. Jesus used these five stages, and they are the same stages that should be used by all leaders who want to successfully engage their followers in a highly meaningful way.

Nevertheless, Jesus also provided us with some additional suggestions and guidelines for maintaining the enabling process. For example, Jesus *met separately with senior apostles.* Such was the way of the man called Jesus—to counsel and advise and to inform his closest assistants about privileged and sacred ideas in private. Jesus trusted his followers and communicated with them. The scriptures recorded frequently that "Jesus called his disciples unto him, and said . . ." (Matthew 15:32). For example, Luke says that "He took Peter and John and James, and went up into a mountain to pray" (Luke 9:28). These were his closest confidants and assistants. This means that presidency meetings, planning and strategy sessions, and administrative meetings all require bringing together in a small group the key leaders of an organization.

The purpose of these smaller meetings is to review critical issues so that consensus among the key leaders can occur before problems are brought to the larger body of the organization. Those present in smaller groups are freer to discuss problems, share feelings, and analyze positions so that they are involved in the decisions. This assumes that the plans and ways to best achieve the goals are presented to the larger group with unity and direction. These administrative meetings must be open and candid, even revealing "sacred" information and authentic differences; however, out of the administrative meetings should evolve a sense of unity and consensus.

When you share special insights with your key leaders, they become more motivated and are able to grasp the deeper meanings and directions that elevate organizational decisions and opportunities.

Jesus also sought new talent and additional leaders. One of the important tasks of a leader is to identify and select other leaders. A leader should select strong associates to guide the organization. Jesus prayerfully searched for those who would become a faithful part of the organization and strengthen the members. "Therefore said he unto them, the harvest truly is great, but the laborers are few: pray ye therefore the Lord of the harvest, that he would send forth laborers into his harvest" Luke 10:2).

Involving others in the work is an obvious leadership imperative. Followers who are involved in the work create enormous amounts of energy that propel others toward achieving the vision. Jesus included his followers in the process of spreading the Gospel. The Savior (1) selected those who would help him, (2) gave them important and specific things to do, (3) instructed and advised them on how to carry out their assignments, and (4) taught them the importance of accountability.

Work organizations, family organizations, and church organizations are formed, primarily, because one person acting alone can never accomplish complex goals that involve large numbers of tasks.

In a university business management class, a professor reminds students that by themselves they will accomplish far less than if they work with others, especially those who want to help in the development and implementation of a product or service.

He further explains that everyone has a million-dollar idea, but statistically speaking, no one in the class will ever become a millionaire. The reason is that most people will not implement their ideas. They just do not have the encouragement or resources to bring their ideas to market.

The professor tells about his millionaire friend, who is very successful at implementing other people's ideas. The friend says, "Most people smile when they have a good idea, but I smile all the way to the bank."

The professor concludes that, in most circumstances, it is much wiser to share ideas, the work associated with implementing a good idea, and the rewards that result. It is better to have 10 per cent of something than 100 per cent of nothing.

A Simple Example of the Sharing Process

The quickest and most complete way to involve people and enable them to act is to share meaningful tasks with them.

If you want to share work in a way that motivates individuals to follow through properly, to feel accountable, you should use a simple seven-step procedure. This process is easiest to visualize if you identify a specific individual with whom you would like to share an assignment, then do the following:

1. Give the Whole Picture. Explain the setting and circumstances under which the shared work will take place. For example, say, "We will be taking 15 minutes to commemorate the restoration of the Aaronic Priesthood at the beginning of our priesthood meeting Sunday. There will be three five-minute talks, and then we will separate into quorums."

2. Describe the Need. You might explain that "the first speaker will be the bishop, after which the teacher's quorum president will speak. What we really need in order to complete the program is a Father who will share something that his family does together that builds family unity."

3. Ask for Suggestions. Ask the father, "What have you done recently that seems to be something that your family enjoys?" The answer from one father was that they had all purchased skiing equipment and were having quite a good time learning to ski. Ask the father, "Do you think you could share that idea with us this Sunday for about 4–5 minutes?"

4. Emphasize the Importance. Be sure to stress the importance of what you are asking the person to do. "The fathers and sons are interested in what your family is doing because they admire how happily your family lives together. And you will be representing all the fathers of the ward."

5. Establish a Trigger Point. Set a time, usually the day before the assignment is to be completed, when the individual can be called, reminded, and encouraged about the assignment. If you are a busy leader, you should assign a secretary or assistant to make the call. Set a time that is convenient to call the individual. Inquire, "How is that talk coming for tomorrow in priesthood meeting? Is there anything further that you need to know about the meeting tomorrow?"

6. Follow Up. Either you or an assistant should make special note of how the assignment was handled. Be sure to give the individual an opportunity to report to you, just as Jesus did with his apostles, about the meeting and his particular assignment.

7. Give Recognition. No matter how many times a person does a task or special assignment, take the time to acknowledge and confirm what the person did. For example, the father who gave the talk was presented a beautiful picture of the restoration of the Aaronic Priesthood with an expression of appreciation from the bishop.

Keeping Everyone Involved

Enabling others demonstrates the trust and confidence leaders have in their followers. Involving others gives the individual an opportunity to develop important capabilities and to increase their knowledge. Involvement usually improves follower's morale and increases commitment because it allows them to help decide how to complete the work.

Regularly invite people to be involved. Do more than just delegate routine tasks. Sometimes it is more encouraging and exciting for an individual to research an idea and write a report. If one of your followers looks a little bored, assign the person to explore a new approach to getting the work done or completing an assignment, and to prepare some advice on the matter.

The point is that as a leader, you need to keep people moving and contributing. Once followers feel a lack of forward motion, they quickly become bored and less productive. You can not afford to wait around until followers energize themselves. You must use every means possible to keep followers involved and on fire.

Although Jesus was able to perform miracles directly, he often involved the person to be healed in the process. For example, Jesus healed a blind person by making clay out of spittle and dirt and anointed the eyes of the blind person. "And said unto him, Go, wash in the pool of Siloam. He went his way therefore, and washed, and came seeing" (John 9: 6–7). In addition, Peter was invited to walk on the sea. To accomplish this feat, the scriptures record that Jesus said, "Come," and when he came down from the ship, he walked on the water (see Matthew 14:22–36). As a leader you must constantly ask people to be part of the process, to join in accomplishing goals and completing the work. Take the initiative to invite those around you to be involved.

At the feeding of the five thousand, Jesus blessed the food, then "gave the loaves to his disciples, and the disciples to the multitude" (Matthew 14:19). An orderly process of involvement was used, with the disciples taking an active role in the miracle. In addition, as Mark explained, a large number of people were organized and given assignments: "And he commanded them to make all sit down by companies upon the green grass. And they sat down in ranks, by hundreds, and by fifties" (Mark 6:39–40).

Great leaders devise ways to involve their followers in accomplishing assignments. For example, in your family, church leadership role, or at work, you need to make certain that everyone has a part in what is happening. Although the specific figures of 50s and 100s are not important, the critical concern is to have a clear system for involving people in the work

There is no better way to learn and become committed to an idea than to experience it for yourself. The successful completion of a task or an activity is what impels and motivates outstanding achievement. Jesus constantly involved others in every possible situation by giving them opportunities to succeed.

For example, the second feeding of a large multitude of people was handled in approximately the same way as the first feeding of five thousand. Jesus called his disciples around him. He explained that he did not want the crowd to be sent away without eating.

He asked the disciples how many loaves of bread and how much other food they had.

He directed the multitude to sit on the ground.

He blessed the food, and "gave to his disciples, and the disciples to the multitude" (Matthew 15:36). Jesus taught the disciples through involving them personally in the work.

The incident involving tribute payment in Capernaum instructs us in ways to engage people by giving them specific assignments:

> And when they were come to Capernaum, they that received tribute money came to Peter, and said, Doth not your master pay tribute? He saith, Yes. And when he was come into the house, Jesus prevented him, saying, What thinkest thou, Simon? of whom do the kings of the earth take custom or tribute? of their own children, or of strangers? Jesus saith unto him, Then are the children free. Notwithstanding, lest we should offend them, go thou to the sea, and cast an hook, and take up the fish that first cometh up; and when thou hast opened his mouth, thou shalt find a piece of money: that take, and give unto them for me and thee. (Matthew 17:27–27)

Jesus could have provided the coin without the intense involvement of Peter—getting his fishing gear, catching a fish, finding the coin, taking it to the tax collector. However, Peter learned from the experience, and his faith was strengthened.

An older home teacher asked his young companion to offer a prayer at the beginning of their visit. As soon as he became comfortable with praying, the senior companion asked him to give a short part of the message to each family whom they were scheduled to visit.

Soon the younger companion became confident and learned how to pray with the families and give lessons. The elder man asked his companion to schedule appointments and to ask the head of each household what message or assistance would be most appropriate for the home teachers to give to the family.

"Success breeds success." "Inch by inch, life's a cinch." These sayings express exactly what happened when the senior home teacher invited and helped his younger companion to succeed. In no time this young Aaronic Priesthood holder was bragging a little to his quorum buddies that "home teaching is a piece of cake if you know what you are doing."

Stimulate and Provoke Others

Involvement consists of much more than encouraging and inviting others to participate in activities. Involvement has an emotional side to it that implores analysis. To be involved is to "feel" the challenge and the excitement of an event. Emotions are stimulated, and participants are carried forward into action.

Jesus suggested this point, somewhat indirectly, when he asked the disciples this question: "Suppose ye that I am come to give peace on earth? I tell you, Nay: but rather division" (Luke 12:51).

Jesus was involving in his approach. He challenged traditions and, as illustrated in the hearing with Pilate, he was criticized with the comment that "He stirreth up the people." Jesus was constantly stimulating and provoking people to keep moving.

Jesus asked for strong commitments, of course, and we should do the same. "So likewise whosoever of you that forsaketh not all that he hath, he cannot be my disciple" (Luke 14:33). This suggests that you should have plans, goals, and expectations.

Kept appointments or completed assignments demonstrate commitment. Jesus taught, "No man, having put his hand to the plough, and looking back, is fit for the kingdom of God" (Luke 9:62). Once you have decided to complete a task, give everything you have to accomplish it.

From time to time, some of Jesus' would-be followers came and went. John reports that "from that time many of his disciples went back, and walked no more with him."

Even the twelve apostles were questioned about their loyalty: "Then said Jesus unto the twelve, Will ye also go away?" The impetuous Peter immediately declared, "Lord, to whom shall we go? thou hast the words of eternal life" (John 6:66–68). These words imply that you must have an impelling vision and powerful goals in order to keep the commitment of those with whom you work. You must also work closely with your followers to be inspiring.

Stay Close

Jesus and his disciples walked together, worked together, ate together, shared experiences together, and encouraged one another.

Throughout the scriptures we read phrases such as

> And both Jesus was called, and his disciples, to the marriage. (John 2:2)

> After this he went down to Capernaum, he, and his mother, and his brethren, and his disciples. (John 2:12)

> After these things came Jesus and his disciples into the land of Judea. (John 3:22)

> And Jesus went up into a mountain, and there he sat with his disciples. (John 6:3)

> Jesus therefore walked no more openly among the Jews; but went thence unto a country near to the wilderness, into a city called Ephraim, and there continued with his disciples. (John 11:54)

Even though the customs of that time did not encourage much socializing between men and women, Jesus was equally comfortable with both. Males and females alike sought instruction from him and could speak to him with ease.

He was quite friendly with the innocent little children. Although he was a Jew, he found good in the Samaritan and faith in the Roman Centurion (Matthew 8:10). Social status and class rank did not matter. Jesus stayed close to his followers, especially his designated twelve apostles.

Jesus frequently talked with his disciples apart from the rest of the multitude. He was no doubt advising, teaching, and admonishing. His task was to help them develop the knowledge, skills, and attitudes necessary to carry on the work.

In training his twelve apostles, Christ had to prepare them for a tempest of opposition and rejection, as well as teach them how to succeed by drawing upon inner power. The disciples would be persecuted, face ostracism, be brought to trial, and be hated by many (Mark 13:9–13). They needed the ability and strength to continue forward even when their leader was not with them. Jesus was definitely not a long-distance leader or an absentee manager. He constantly directed and supported his followers.

As a leader, it is your task to help develop the people with whom you work. This should happen as you meet, teach, advise, and express adequate appreciation to them.

This point may be illustrated by a discussion among a group of students studying important leadership skills that managers should know. Management by objectives (MBO) was mentioned. A student mentioned management by walking around (MBWA). Soon everyone caught the spirit and began using similar abbreviations like MBTAI for management by talking about it, and MBTP for management by thinking positively.

Near the conclusion of this creative sojourn into the realms of humanistic leadership, a student who had been reading about the life of Christ suggested that you would not be following Jesus' example of leadership unless you LBET, lead by eating together.

After a round of youthful laughter, the would-be scholars agreed that Christ enhanced his leadership success by working, walking, eating, talking, and probably sharing some humor about the daily happenings in Jerusalem with his followers.

For parents as leaders, sometimes the only way to direct a teenager is to talk together while working on a project or sharing insights while eating someplace.

Leaders, who share a meal or conversation with their followers, are not surprised at the understanding, trust, and loyalty that develop from such simple activities.

The greatest lesson of close leadership is illustrated by last days of Jesus' life, when he sat with the apostles during the Passover. Luke explained that "there was also a strife among them, which of them should be accounted the greatest" (Luke 22:24).

In response to the bickering, Jesus explained the philosophy of leadership that underlies this key:

> The kings of the Gentiles exercise lordship over them;
> and they that exercise authority upon them are called
> benefactors. But ye shall not be so: but he that is great-
> est among you, let him be the younger; and he that is
> chief, as he that doth serve. (Luke 22:27)

Great leaders do not dominate their followers. Rather they set directions and tone, while stimulating enthusiasm and involvement. The purest leader is one who can envision the future of a group or organization. She can attract others to participate as well as build their talents and abilities to achieve the vision.

You may have noticed that Jesus favored inviting and enabling his followers rather than telling and empowering. And you may have also noticed that we have avoided trying to explain theories of motivation. The reason is simple: it is much more human and ennobling to ask and invite people to do things than it is to tell them.

Japanese managers feel that they have failed if they have to tell or command someone to do something. We believe that they are right. All of us need to reexamine our language usage when involving and enabling others. Perhaps we would all be more effective if we used words like "could you?" "would you?" and "can you?" rather than "do this" and "do that."

Listening to the conversations about assignments in a productive company called Chemical & Mineralogical Services was more than interesting. Each time the owner/manager needed to have something done, he walked up to an employee and said, "Could you analyze these ore samples first this evening?" Or he asked, "On your way back from lunch would you be able to stop past the chemical supply house and pick up another couple of bottles of acid?" It was amazing the respect that was demonstrated for employees by inviting them to do things rather than giving orders.

This fourth leadership key, argues that, as portrayed by Jesus, you should (1) invite people to be involved, (2) help them feel the involvement, and (3) stay close to them as they are involved. In these ways, you can lead people to exhibit the power and determination to achieve both organizational goals and their own personal work goals.

If you follow this pattern of enabling, you will be considered a person to be followed, a person who has guided fellow employees as well as church and family members in achieving more than was expected. You will be an enabler of followers who has helped them to act in their own self-interest and in the best interest of the organization. Your followers will call you *blessed*, an inspiring leader.

5

THE FIFTH KEY:
STRENGTHEN YOURSELF

Late one afternoon after a work-filled day, Jesus and his disciples boarded a small ship to cross the lake. As the boat set sail, Jesus fell asleep near the ship's stern. "And behold, there arose a great tempest in the sea, insomuch that the ship was covered with the waves, but he was asleep" (Matthew 8:24).

This circumstance, according to Talmage, is most informative because it helps us understand the reality of Jesus' physical attributes and the healthy condition of his body. "He was subject to fatigue and bodily exhaustion from other causes, as are all men; without food he grew hungry; without drink He thirsted; by labor He became weary" (Talmage, 307).

Good Health was Important to Jesus

The fact that after a day of strenuous effort He could calmly sleep, even amid the turmoil of a tempest, indicates an unimpaired nervous system and a good state of health. Nowhere do we find a record of Jesus having been ill. He lived according to the laws of health, yet never allowed the body to rule the spirit.

His daily activities made heavy demands on both his physical and mental energies. They were met with neither symptoms of nervous collapse nor of functional disturbance. Sleep after toil is natural and necessary. "The day's work done, Jesus slept."

To lead others tirelessly, patiently, and effectively, through periods of disappointment and fatigue, requires that you master the basic principles of personal regeneration and self-renewal.

Absolutely nothing in scriptural records allows us to imagine Jesus as a sad, gloomy, fatigued, depressed, and overburdened person. It is equally impossible to try to picture Jesus with his robes flying outward behind him, rushing thither and yon, helter-skelter, trying to accomplish twenty things at one time.

Although we see many young business leaders and parents looking a bit disheveled as they rush through their daily agendas, you may rest assured that they are not following the strong, calm, and steady example set by the Man from Galilee.

Though Jesus' life was dedicated to serving and leading people, he did not ignore the opportunity to relax with friends, eat nourishing food, and sleep after a day of work.

Observance of the laws of health, together with the proper use of faith and prayer, will do much to lift your spirits. Finding joy in attending to peoples' special needs, resisting the appearance of busyness, and concentrating on one thing at a time will help you to renew your own inner strength.

Keep the Laws of Health

Throughout the scriptures we are instructed concerning appropriate health practices. Adam was introduced to the best use of crops and herbs (Genesis 1:29–36). Noah and Moses were given enlightenment about various herbs and meats (Genesis 9:3–4; Deuteronomy 14:2–3). Daniel and his companions received special direction about what to eat in the house of the King of Babylon (Daniel 1).

A section of the Doctrine and Covenants, frequently referred to as "the word of wisdom," provides some principles of health and well-being that are useful to all of us in strengthening our physical stature. Jesus is quoted in Section 88, saying, "Cease to be idle; cease to sleep longer than is needful; retire to they bed early, they ye may not be weary; arise early, that your bodies and your minds may be invigorated."

These scriptures give only a general outline of things you should do to strengthen yourself physically. Another section, however, describes more specific practices having to do with what to eat, drink, and generally take into our bodies in order to develop strength. In Section 89, Jesus explains quite directly that "strong drinks are not for the belly, but for the washing of your bodies." He continues to explain that "tobacco is not for the body, neither for the belly, and is not good for man, but is an herb for bruises and all sick cattle, to be used with judgment and skill."

Contemporary researchers worldwide support that advice, especially concerning the use of tobacco. There is also great concern about "hot drinks," which are interpreted nowadays to mean alcoholic and caffeine products. Their abuse is a continuing issue among health experts, as well as the general public. It seems clear that alcohol and tobacco are not good for people if they seek to have good health. To be wise in what you consume, you should abstain from alcohol, tobacco, and other drug related products.

Jesus gives additional advice in this same section concerning other foods. He says that "all wholesome herbs God hath ordained for the constitution, nature, and use of man, every herb in the season thereof, and every fruit in the season thereof; all these to be used with prudence and thanksgiving." He also explains that "all grain is ordained for the use of man and of beasts, to be the staff of life. Nevertheless, wheat is for man, and corn for the ox, and oats for the horse, and rye for the fowls and for swine, and barley for all useful animals and for mild drinks, as also other grain."

He also comments on the use of meat: "flesh also of beasts and of the fowls of the air, I have ordained for the use of man with thanksgiving; nevertheless they are to be used sparingly." This advice suggests that eating meat infrequently is a good idea, and that grains are especially good for our health.

Many experts have recently recognized the very close connection between good health and both physical and mental functioning. There appears to be an interesting relationship between our minds and our bodies. Psychological textbooks and other writings often refer to "physiological psychology," or "psychological physiology." The essence of these writings is that our physical health has a direct impact on our mental health. If you are going to be an effective leader, you must take care of your physical health in order to function well mentally.

Former President Ezra Taft Benson observed that "rest and physical exercise are essential, and a walk in the fresh air can refresh our spirit. Wholesome recreation and a change of pace is necessary, and even its anticipation can lift the spirit" (in *Conference Report*, October 1974, 92). This comment clearly suggests that regular recreation is important in keeping healthy, that even a vacation from time to time may also contribute to your well-being.

Nevertheless, adherence to principles expressed in the "word of wisdom" may have additional salutary effects that go beyond simple good physical health. Elder Stephen L. Richards, when a member of the Quorum of the Twelve Apostles explained that "the largest measure of good derived from its [the word of wisdom] observance is an increased faith and the development of more spiritual power and wisdom" (in *Conference Report*, Apr. 1949, 141). We shall address this issue next and attempt to point out how strengthening faith can also make you a more effective leader.

Use Your Faith

Faith helps us to overcome difficulties. It controls doubts and fears that we sometimes experience when we are trying to lead effectively.

Jesus assured us of the powerful possibilities of faith when he said, "Verily I say unto you, If ye have faith as a grain of mustard seed, ye shall say unto this mountain, Remove hence to yonder place; and it shall remove; and nothing shall be impossible unto you" (Matthew 17:20).

The literal meaning of this statement is stunning. To think that just a little bit of faith could move something as large as a mountain staggers the mind. In addition, if we accept the figurative idea of "moving a mountain" to mean to overcome a major difficulty, it is equally awesome to imagine that a miniscule amount of faith can lead you to achieve great feats.

The New Testament is replete with stories of Jesus' ability to remain calm and in control while dealing with difficult situations; however, few insights are more instructive than Jesus stilling the storms as recorded in Matthew.

During the evening, Jesus and his disciples entered a ship that was sailing across the Sea of Galilee toward the far shore. A storm started and quickly increased in fury. The small ship was tossed about mercilessly upon the waves until the water started coming in, over the sides. Jesus seemed to be resting peacefully.

Though the disciples had grown up in the area and were well acquainted with the sudden storms and wind-lashed waves of this body of water, they became frightened. At last, with each moment literally threatening their utter destruction, they went to the stern of the ship and awakened Jesus with the cry: "Lord, save us: we perish" (Matthew 8:25).

Without alarm and with amazing self-control, Jesus quietly appraised the situation. His only question was "Why are ye fearful, O ye of little faith?" "Then, he arose and rebuked the winds and the sea; and there was a great calm" (Matthew 8:26).

On a later occasion Jesus crossed the waters again in a small boat to escape the crowds, find seclusion, and seek a time to rest. The departure of Jesus and the Twelve had been observed by an enthusiastic crowd of five thousand. They ran along the shore, around the end of the lake, and finally arrived at the landing place.

Jesus and his companions "had compassion on them," taught them, and administered to their afflictions. In the late hours of the day, Jesus performed the miracle of the loaves and fishes, fed the multitude, and even gathered twelve baskets of surplus.

Jubilant, the crowds proposed proclaiming Jesus their King. Knowing their intentions and realizing that his whole Messianic mission could be thwarted in one short moment, Jesus requested that His disciples leave by boat while he stayed and dispersed the excited crowd.

After his chosen disciples were safely journeying across the lake, Jesus cleared up the crowd's misconceptions. Then he ascended a hill and secluded Himself in prayer during most of the night.

As fate would have it, the disciples' boat trip met with near disaster. "The ship was now in the midst of the sea, tossed with waves and the wind was contrary" (Matthew 14:24). The crew labored hard most of the night to keep the ship from being wrecked, but they made very little progress on their course.

Jesus, though secluded from his disciples, knew of their perilous plight. The scriptural records describe what happened next: "And in the fourth watch of the night Jesus went unto them, walking on the sea. And when the disciples saw him walking on the sea, they were troubled, saying, It is a spirit; and they cried out for fear. But straightway Jesus spake unto them, saying, Be of good cheer; it is I; be not afraid."

"And Peter answered him and said, Lord, if it be thou, bid me come unto thee on the water. And he said, Come. And when Peter was come down out of the ship, he walked on the water, to go to Jesus, But when he saw the wind boisterous, he was afraid; and beginning to sink, he cried, saying, Lord, save me. And immediately Jesus stretched forth his hand, and caught him, and said unto him, O thou of little faith, wherefore didst thou doubt? And when they were come into the ship, the wind ceased" (Matthew 14:25–32).

These marvelous demonstrations of faith show us that even natural forces can be controlled with great spiritual power. Of equal importance is Peter's remarkable experience.

Although he was usually somewhat impetuous, Peter is to be commended for at least trying to duplicate the miraculous feat of his Master. Peter requested the opportunity to walk on the waves. Jesus assented and invited him to "Come."

The scriptures record, "He walked on the water." But, then in a moment of rationality he realized the enormity of what he was able to do and began to sink.

Peter showed that with sufficient faith, walking on water could be done. Had his faith not wavered when hit by the wind sweeping across the turbulent water, Peter may have reached Jesus. You, like Peter, can use your faith to become a more effective leader. We want to tell you a story about two young men who used faith to bring about a simple but profound effect.

Two missionaries in the Samoan Islands were preparing for a meeting with some potential converts. Having felt the spirit during previous visits with each family, they invited them to come and hear the message of the Gospel, and ask questions about the Church of Jesus Christ of Latter-day Saints.

At that time, ministers from some other churches in the village sent out word that members of their congregations were to deny the missionaries from entering their homes. The people were also forbidden to attend any meetings under the direction of the missionaries.

The missionaries felt that it was their duty to let all the villagers know that Jesus' message was true and that baptism could only be administered by those who held the proper authority. So the missionaries decided to approach each house one at a time and invite every family to attend a meeting anyway.

The Samoan homes were oval-shaped, with poles set in the ground to support the roof. The poles were spaced four or five feet apart and capped with a dome-shaped thatched roof. During the day, the walls, which consisted of thatched leaf blinds, were pulled up so as to expose most of the activities inside the house.

So even though the missionaries were sometimes not invited into the house, they were able to deliver their message to the parents and children who were seated inside.

The missionaries aroused considerable curiosity about the meeting, and when the appointed hour arrived for the meeting to begin, the meetinghouse was filled to capacity.

The meeting place was about the size of several native houses, but instead of a thatched roof, the roof was composed of sheets of tin covering the layer of woven leaves.

As the meeting began, it started to rain. Samoa receives some of the heaviest rains in the world. When a rain comes, it is like someone turning on a million water faucets. The force of the rain hitting the roof was awesome, but the sound was worse.

The large raindrops splattering on the tin roof was similar to hundreds of drumsticks playing a drum roll on top of a giant tin can. The sound was so loud that it stopped the meeting. No one could hear the message of the young missionaries.

Some people in attendance thought that the interruption was providential, and a possible warning to disband the meeting and return home. The missionary who was conducting the meeting waited for a short time to see if the rain would stop. It did not.

As the noisy rain continued, the audience became more restless and started making plans to leave. The missionaries were now visibly shaken, feeling that they had overcome great odds and spent much time arranging for the meeting, only to have their plans ruined by the noise of the rain.

For a few minutes, the two missionaries discussed the gravity of the situation. They had great faith in Jesus, and wanted to proclaim his message to this group of Samoans. They had recently been taught by President David O. McKay that "man's extremity is the Lord's opportunity." They believed that if they went as far as they could to render service or preach the Gospel, and were confronted by an impending obstacle, a way would be opened to complete the task.

With considerable fear and trembling, the more experienced missionary quietly stepped outside under the eave of the roof. The rain was coming down in torrents, literally in walls of huge drops, pounding and rattling the metal roof.

Humbly and undaunted, the missionary raised his arms and ask for the rain to stop. In his own human way, he explained all the visits and conversations they had in getting people out to the meeting. He said that he did not know what to do, and that it was now in the Lord's hands. Before the missionary could step back into the meeting place, the rain stopped and the noise ceased.

Unquestionably, faith is a principle of power, a gift that all should cultivate. For leaders, it provides another way to bless people's lives, remove obstacles, and strengthen themselves.

Joseph Smith teaches in the *Lectures on Faith* that "when a man works by faith he works by mental exertion instead of physical force" (Smith, 61).

The mind is the essential part of us that perceives, feels, thinks, and wills. We exercise faith by willing and strongly desiring something good and right to happen.

Every valiant leader has feelings of frustration and fatigue. When almost overcome with a never-ending struggle, every adult seeks refuge from the storm. To those who toil with faith, the promise is given: "Ask and it shall be given you; seek, and ye shall find; knock and it shall be opened unto you" (Matthew 7:7).

That is a real promise packed with power. If we ask with a sincere heart, real intent, and having faith, we will be strengthened.

As with Peter and other faithful disciples, while in the midst of the worst imaginable circumstances, so we can be reassured by the comforting voice of Jesus saying, "Be of good cheer; it is I; be not afraid."

Don't Be Afraid to Pray and Ponder

Jesus told his apostles that to have faith sufficiently strong to cast out devils requires the addition of fasting and prayer (Mark 9:14–29).

James E. Talmage, author of one of the most scholarly works on the life of Jesus, indicates that prayer, fasting, and faith are related. He explains that faith can be used to personally strengthen and benefit oneself, but prayer must eventually be added to the formula:

> The Savior's statement concerning the evil spirit that the apostles were unable to subdue—"Howbeit this kind goeth not out but by prayer and fasting"—indicates gradation in the malignity and evil power of demons, and gradation also in the results of varying degrees of faith. The apostles who failed on the occasion referred to had been able to cast out demons at other times. Fasting, when practiced in prudence, and genuine prayer are conducive to the development of faith with its accompanying power for good. Individual application of this principle may be made with profit. Have you some besetting weakness, some sinful indulgence that you have vainly tried to overcome? Like the malignant demon that Christ rebuked in the boy, your sin may be of a kind that goeth out only through prayer and fasting. (Talmage, 1973, 395)

Leaders have always found time for meditation and prayer. Jesus was not different. His entire ministry was punctuated with moments spent away from the crowds and his chosen disciples. He prayed, pondered his mission, and received great spiritual strength.

Although Jesus knew the purpose of his work and the direction he should go, he nevertheless prayed constantly. For example, after feeding five thousand and before rescuing his frightened disciples from a capsizing boat, Matthew records that Jesus "sent the multitudes away, he went up into a mountain apart to pray: and when the evening was come, he was there alone" (Matthew 14:23).

Jesus must have prayed several hours. He probably prayed for his followers, who were soon to be asked, "Whom say ye that I am?" He wanted them to survive every challenge and crisis, for he knew that they would have to lead at the moment of his departure.

During his hours of prayer Jesus was impressed by the impending disaster facing his disciples. So "in the fourth watch of the night, Jesus went unto them, walking on the sea" (Matthew 14:25).

Christ was concerned enough to walk directly across the water to the boat rather than take the more indirect route around the coastline.

Clearly Christ's impressions about the boat's impending crisis and his decision to help the disciples occurred during an intense period of prayer. Although the first plan was to meet the boat on the opposite shore, Jesus was prayerfully inspired to walk directly to the sea-bound vessel.

Renewed Strength Comes through Prayer

Marion G. Romney, former counselor in the First Presidency, speaking of the Savior's life and example, concluded by saying, "Finally, and most importantly, I learned that he communed constantly with his Father through prayer. This he did not only to learn the will of his Father, but also to obtain the strength to do his Father's will" (Romney, September 1972, 5).

Praying to learn the will of Heavenly Father and then asking for the strength to press forward even when the day is long and the work is hard is one of the ways that Jesus was able to strengthen and renew himself.

Luke records that between the commotion caused by Jesus healing a man on the Sabbath, whose right hand was withered, and the task of choosing twelve apostles from among his disciples, Jesus went out into a mountain to pray, and continued all night in prayer to God. Renewed and refreshed when the daylight came, Jesus called all his disciples to him and chose twelve, whom he named Apostles.

Then he came down with them and met a great multitude of people from Judea and Jerusalem. He spent the entire day teaching them and healing those who had diseases (Luke 6:6–13).

What an incredible series of events compressed into such a short period of time. Yet Jesus had the insight and strength to carry on important activities all day, all night, and all the following day.

In a quorum meeting, a Melchizedek priesthood holder, when asked to describe what he did to keep himself close to the Lord, explained: "The single, most effective thing that I do to stay close to the Lord, beyond trying to keep the commandments, is to pray twice before I go to work in the morning." His first sentence, phrased rather simply, seemed to capture everyone's interest.

He explained that he usually arose, before anyone else in his family, between 5:30 and 6:00 A.M. in the morning. He quietly slipped into the bathroom to shave and made sure his eyes were partially open so that he wouldn't cut himself. After shaving, he flossed and brushed his teeth and immediately before showering, knelt in prayer. He said that he always whispered his prayer loud enough so that he could hear what he was saying.

> The fullness of my heart was overflowing. I was so grateful to be alive and to have the comfort and guidance that the Gospel brings. My prayer was usually over in about forty-five seconds to a minute, but it seemed like an hour. I expressed deep appreciation for the consciousness of life that is in me and the opportunity to engage in the day's activities. Most important, I reviewed two or three things that I wanted to accomplish before the day ended, tasks beyond those that were expected of me, and prayed for the necessary strength to accomplish them. For example, I need to fill all of my assignments connected with teaching at the university, but I also wanted to finish writing a chapter for a new book and to make arrangements for a management seminar for an out-of-state nursing association. When I finish saying my first prayer, I have a relaxing, warm shower and review the activities of the day. Often in this calm condition, I receive insights into what should be said or done to make each activity of the day go more smoothly. After a pleasant shower, I go into my closet to get dressed. Once again, I kneel down and whisper a prayer. This second prayer is done to see if I can even remember what I asked about in the first one. I feel strongly that I have often prayed and then forgotten what I prayed about. In this way, I become more committed to what I truly want to accomplish during the day. I leave the closet with the strength and encouragement to move ahead with confidence. When I leave the house in the morning, I actually look forward with anticipation to a prayer of appreciation in the evening for the strength and encouragement received during the day.

During the hours of the Savior's greatest agony, he found a place of seclusion in the Garden of Gethsemane. He had been there before. His disciples followed him.

Jesus said unto them, "Pray that ye enter not into temptation."

Then he withdrew from them, kneeled down, and prayed, saying, "Father, if thou be willing, remove this cup from me; nevertheless, not my will, but thine be done." His Father's will was done, but Luke tells us that in response to His prayer, "there appeared an Angel unto him, strengthening him." (Luke 22:43)

Clear Impressions Come When You are Relaxed

The efficacy of Jesus' example of prayer and the spirit of communion manifest in Jesus' daily life is further detailed by a remarkable experience related by President David O. McKay to the quorum of the Twelve and retold by President Harold B. Lee:

> A few weeks ago, President McKay related to the Twelve an interesting experience, and I asked him yesterday if I might repeat it to you this morning. He said, "It is a great thing to be responsive to the whisperings of the spirit, and we know that when these whisperings come, it is a gift and our privilege to have them. They come when we are relaxed and not under pressure of appointments." I want you to mark that. The President then took occasion to relate an experience in the life of Bishop John Wells, former member of the Presiding Bishopric. Brother John Wells was a great detail man and prepared many of the reports we are following up now. His boy was run over by a freight train. Sister Wells was inconsolable. She mourned during the three days prior to the funeral, received no comfort at the funeral, and was in a rather serious state of mind. One day soon after the funeral services, while she was lying on her bed, relaxed, still mourning, she says that her son appeared to her and said, "Mother, do not mourn, do not cry. I am alright." He told her that she did not understand how the accident happened and explained that he had given the signal to the engineer to move on, and then made the usual effort to catch the railing on the freight train. It was clearly an accident. Now listen! He said that as soon as he realized that he was in another environment, he tried to see his father, *but*

he couldn't reach him. His father was so busy with the duties in his office, he could not respond to his call. Therefore, he had come to his mother. He said to her, "You tell father that all is well with me, and I want you not to mourn anymore."

The President made the statement that the point he had in mind was that when we are relaxed, in a private room, we are more susceptible to those things, and that, so far as he was concerned, his best thoughts come after he gets up in the morning and is relaxed and thinking about the duties of the day; that impressions come more clearly, as if it were to hear a voice. Those impressions are right. If we are worried about something and upset in our feelings, the inspiration does not come. If we so live that our minds are free from worry and our conscience is clear and our feelings are right toward one another, the operation of the spirit of the Lord upon our spirit is as real as when we pick up the telephone; but when they come, we must be brave enough to take the suggested actions. The Lord will approve it and the brethren will approve it, and we know it is right. He said, "It is a great consolation in this upset world today to know that our Savior is directing this work." Then the President concluded: "I value that testimony. If you forget all else I have said, you remember that lesson and admonition." (Lee, 1956)

Let us reiterate the three key points made by this incident.

First, you must feel calm and relaxed. Your mind cannot be filled with noise and chatter that blocks inspiration when it comes.

Second, you must feel right toward others. If you are upset with our family members, leaders at work, or neighbors, it is difficult to allow the subtle inspiration to come.

And, third, you must be seeking direction, or as President David O. McKay explained, be "thinking about the duties of the day." To let a concern or thought rest lightly upon the mind allows "impressions to come more clearly, as if to hear a voice."

Sometimes inspiration comes in the morning. Other times it comes during the quiet evening hours. The location may also vary. Leaders have received inspiration walking the beaches of Hawaii, viewing the sites of Ancient Jerusalem, and sitting under the tall pines of a national forest. It is most important for you to keep calm and be receptive to the inspiration.

Focus on Results, Not Procedures

Jesus often set aside the narrow forms and practices of the Pharisees. He constantly de-emphasized the letter of the law and gave renewed life to the spirit of the law. "Walk so far on the Sabbath," said the rule and tradition. Jesus walked as far as he needed. "Pray in this way and in these public places." Jesus was outraged. He pleaded, "Pray to the Father which is in secret; and thy Father which seeth in secret shall reward thee openly" (Matthew 6:5–8).

"Eat these things and these you shall not," said the Code. Knowing that certain foods were good for the body, Jesus pointed out a greater truth: "Not that which goeth into the mouth defileth a man; but that which cometh out of the mouth, this defileth a man" (Matthew 15:11).

There are very few instances in which the Lord prescribes specific procedures for accomplishing a significant outcome. Keeping the Sabbath day holy is a guideline without a long list of do's and don'ts. Honor Thy Father and Thy Mother is a great principle with a wonderful promise, "that thy days may be long upon the earth." But no extensive list of practices and procedures is given to implement the principle.

Leaders find themselves in a multitude of meetings. Each meeting should have a separate and distinct purpose. The achievement of the purpose or the outcome of the meeting is much more important than the exact procedure used. The meeting length, number of agenda items, and the order of reports are not as critical as accomplishing the purpose of the meeting.

To be a great leader, you should focus on achieving results, not on conducting a particular number of meetings or on using some specific procedures. Effective leadership is measured by the quality of results achieved, not by the amount of effort expended. As a leader you need to be especially careful about applying rigid programs and procedures in the same way to all of your followers. Each lesson, program, and general policy should be adapted to produce the greatest benefit for the person to whom it is being applied. Modifications and minor adjustments are usually necessary.

A leader is a sign of hope whose ideas are worth following. If a leader feels that his main goal is to complete a specific number of meetings, the experience of being a leader is likely to be somewhat depressing.

On the contrary, if a leader sees a particular meeting as an opportunity to attend to the needs of various people, encourage them, and give them, even in a large meeting, information that allows them to be happier and more successful during the coming week, then the leader and the followers are lifted up and rejoice together.

The leader's goal should be to help people achieve something, not just hold a meeting, conduct an interview, or make a visit. Jesus, as a great leader, enjoyed walking through fields, clashing wits, eating, and having long conversations with people. Here is the perfect example of a leader "ministering" to people first and "administering" programs and procedures second. Jesus is a leader bearing glad tidings of great joy, bringing good new, and describing a lifestyle calculated to lighten the hearts and minds of all followers.

Robert C. Leslie who wrote a definitive text on Jesus called *Jesus and Logotherapy* grasped the significance of Jesus' leadership approach with two basic observations: that Jesus always made contact with people on a direct, personal level and that Jesus did not minister to individuals in the same, stereotyped way.

Jesus' personalized approach "is the most characteristic trait" in his life and style. Again and again he singled out individuals and related to them. He even sensed one woman touching him in a crowd. Jesus noticed Zacchaeus in a crowd and called him by name.

Jesus followed no pattern as he responded to individuals. He did not depend on any particular technique or way to deal with people. He improvised in almost every instance so as to use the resources immediately available to acknowledge and assist individual followers. In fact, he used the most natural and, seemingly, most appropriate ways to engage individuals.

Jesus gives us an excellent example of how to adapt a vast number of explicit policies and procedures to the needs of individual followers. By the time Jesus came into the world, the original Ten Commandments had been elaborated and specified into a horrendous number of detailed restrictions, limitations, and explanations. Religious leaders of his time took great pride in enforcing the unnecessary minutiae uniformly on all residents of the area.

We are certain that Jesus felt that individuals were so distracted from the original commandments by the minutiae that they had drifted away from them. Thus, Matthew recounts the meeting of Jesus with some Pharisees, among whom was a lawyer trying to trick him into identifying which of the hundreds of rules an regulations were the most important. The lawyer "asked him a question, and saying, Master, which is the great commandment in the law? Jesus said unto him, Thou shalt love the Lord they God with all they heart, and with all they soul, and with all they mind. This is the first and great commandment. And the second is like unto it, Thou shalt love they neighbor as thyself. On these two commandments hang all the law and the prophets" (Matthew 22:35–40).

These profound but simple commandments comprehended all of the laws and details and focused the people on two key results: love the Lord and love each other. The people left to implement the two commandments in ways that were consistent with one another but that allowed them to decide for themselves exactly how best to achieve those two goals.

You should do as the man called Jesus did and keep focused on the key outcomes rather than get bogged down in excessive rules, regulations, and policies. Look for results rather than to implement procedures. For example, some universities have attempted to adopt total quality management techniques without realizing that universities are inverted bureaucracies and are not readily amenable to programs implemented from the top down, as TQM should be. The faculty are at the top of the bureaucracy and administrative personnel are at the bottom, making quality measures more appropriate for the administrative employees, but it is the administrative staff who seek to have faculty adopt total quality procedures. The minutiae of total quality processes seldom work well in faculty-student relationships, although TQM is well adapted to improving manufacturing and financial procedures.

The result of these misapplications is a system that is out of sync. The problem is accentuated by today's environment in which new technologies are coming into the work place more rapidly than organizations can adapt to them. In such instances, some managers defer to "old" policy manuals and rigidly enforce procedures that are inappropriate with new ways of doing things. Really competitive companies have essentially abandoned routine procedures and adopted systems that allow orders to be taken and delivered directly from the manufacturing floor to the customer. Such moves demonstrate that leaders must be entirely flexible, operate on the basis of few guidelines, and get to the result as directly as possible.

Leaders must work within the spirit of a policy and adapt to the needs of followers. Because of the widespread concern about the worldwide breakdown of families, a concomitant concern has developed about working mothers. The question is, should mothers be required to stay in the home? Although it is a good idea for children to be cared for and supervised by parents, sensitive employers, members of the community, religious leaders, and administrators of government agencies must provide adaptations of the general philosophy especially for families who may be unable to provide adequate resources without having mothers work outside the home. Thus, special programs for enlisting the support of others to assist with children, sharing jobs, and rotating in and out of the workplace become especially important.

Avoid the Appearance of Busyness

Christ's demeanor was characterized by neither a gloomy face, nor a voice of deep sadness. He never ignored his follower's specific needs, nor did he give them an impression of extreme busyness.

The Gospels record that, with ease, Jesus unhurriedly mingled with large crowds, small children, publicans, outcasts, rich, poor, Pharisees, merchants, and tax collectors.

The scriptures also indicate that he talked with anyone who wanted to discuss points of law, be taught the gospel, or obtain relief from physical affliction.

Jesus seemed to enjoy ministering to the needs of people. At times he was criticized because he found joy and peace in serving and because his disciples did not fast and look appropriately gloomy.

Some scribes and Pharisees murmured against the disciples saying, "Why do ye eat and drink with publicans and sinners?" And questioned Jesus, "Why do the disciples of John fast often, and make prayers, and likewise the disciples of the Pharisees: but thine eat and drink?" (Luke 5:30–35)

Jesus' answer is a marvelous description of how he perceived his own mission. "Can the children of the bride chamber mourn as long as the bridegroom is with them?" (Matthew 9:15) Jesus seems to be saying, "I am the bridegroom. Let us celebrate this moment together and let us be happy now, for there will be sufficient time for solemnity when we are no longer together."

He resisted the appearance of busyness. Nowhere can we find scriptural evidence that Jesus raced from place to place or hurried from one task to another. Indeed, the evidence suggests that the Savior spent time with each person or each group who gathered around him (see Luke 7:36 and Luke 9:12).

When the children swarmed around Jesus, tugging at him and touching him, the disciples thought it was improper and tried to stop them, but Jesus quickly reminded them, "Suffer the little children to come unto me, and forbid them not: for of such is the kingdom of God" (Mark 10:13–14). Jesus had time for the little children.

Christ seems to have set a comfortable but steady pace for accomplishing his work. In modern scriptures the Lord admonishes us not to run faster or labor more than we have the strength for, but to be diligent to the end (see D&C 10:4). Jesus obviously emphasized getting results rather than giving the appearance of busyness. Some leaders mistakenly believe that to be busy is to be effective. These leaders focus on effort rather than on the end result.

An important way to avoid the appearance of being rushed is to allow for extra time to travel to a place or complete a task. For example, you may need to get up a little earlier in the morning in order to groom yourself properly, enjoy some breakfast and drive to your place of employment. The key is to think through what will be happening and leave a little more time so that you will not be rushed. Then move steadily ahead from task to task. Do not allow yourself to be rushed. Enjoy each activity, complete it, and then move immediately to the next one. Rushing from place to place only unsettles your system; it does not keep you focused on achieving results, but it simply infuses into your already crowded schedule additional activity. Always allow more time than you think will be needed to complete something.

The most common situation in which being too rushed is apparent is the first few minutes after arriving at work. You have probably experienced the rush of people flying into your office, the personal contacts that people need to have with you, and the decisions that must be made immediately. In this circumstance, stay calm, take each decision one at a time, complete it, then move on to the next one. Set a comfortable but steady pace and devote only the amount of energy and the amount of time you have for each task. Nevertheless, be diligent to the end. Do not falter and begin to rush aimlessly about the office. Look to complete a task so that you achieve an end result. When you see that you have completed something, you can proceed to the next problem with renewed enthusiasm and confidence.

Enjoy One Thing at a Time

Jesus made many decisions concerning his priorities. Scriptures give strong evidence that he concentrated on, and enjoyed, one task at a time. For example, Luke records that even when a multitude of people pressed him, Jesus was able to perceive that virtue had "gone out of himself" when someone touched him. He asked who it was. Peter said that the crowd was too large to identify one individual who may have approached Jesus and touched the hem of his garment. However, a woman, perceiving that she had been noticed, came trembling before him and confessed that she had touched him and had been immediately healed. Jesus took the time to speak with her, comfort her, and explain that her great faith had healed her.

In a seminar on "Suggestibility and Psychosomatics," in Mission Bay, California, a famous researcher explained that if we would take a moment to relax and think about a glass of water, feel it touching our tongue, taste it, and focus on it going down our throats and refreshing us, the glass of water could be as enjoyable as a serving of turkey or mashed potatoes.

The psychologist further explained that we generally don't think about enjoying a morning stretch, a little conversation, or even the sun on our necks. We are so occupied with going places and doing things that we sometimes fail to enjoy the actual trip or the specific task.

A very busy businessman was making phone calls. He, however, did things a little different than most people who need to make a series of business calls. This individual paused before he called. He thought about whom he was calling and the purpose of the call. He also tried to remember when he had last talked to that person and what kind of opening comments would communicate a feeling of friendlessness and helpfulness.

The businessman seemed quite relaxed and ready to enjoy his call. For a moment, all other calls were forgotten. It was time to be happy, at this moment, with this individual.

Jesus, after he conversed with the woman who had been healed by touching his garment, continued to speak. During the process, he became aware that someone from the house of the ruler of the synagogue said to the ruler, "Thy daughter is dead; trouble not the Master." But when Jesus heard this, he explained that if they believed, she would be made whole.

Then Jesus went to the house and invited Peter, James, John and the maiden's mother and father inside. After some discussion, Jesus invited them to leave, took the maiden by the hand, and said, "Maid, arise." She arose and Jesus asked the parents to give her something to eat (see Luke 8:43–56).

Sometimes we become so busy as leaders that we constantly think about all the things we have to accomplish and fail to enjoy the task at hand. It takes discipline to focus, but, like Jesus, we can render service and truly enjoy each opportunity.

Between the first days of Jesus' ministry, when shouting crowds hailed the new prophet-leader, to the last hours of his mortal agony on the cross, this perfect leader never allowed himself to sink into, or remain in, the dismal abyss of despair and desperation.

Time after time, Jesus was renewed and strengthened by his adherence to laws of health, his magnificent faith, the constant use of prayer, and finding happiness in service by responding to the specific needs of individuals.

You have the same opportunities to be strengthened and renewed as we attempt to influence and lead your family, Church members, neighbors, and co-workers. Your goal is to help all people think more nobly about themselves and reach their highest potentials.

To maintain your strength, hope, and happiness over an extended period of time, you must serve like Jesus, learn more about daily self-renewal, and claim the promises made in Isaiah: "But they that wait upon the Lord shall renew their strength; they shall mount up with wings as eagles; they shall run and not be weary; and they shall walk and not faint" (Isaiah 40:31).

6

MAKING LEADERSHIP EASIER

We have now come full circle in our quest to understand how to become more effective leaders. The ideal leader is Jesus Christ himself, and the ideal leadership style is comprehended in the way Jesus led and influenced his followers. Are you ready to accept the challenge of Jesus to "Come, follow me" and practice his perfect leadership approach at home, at work, in the Church, and in the community?

As we stated earlier, all of us are leaders. Whenever we seek to inspire others to achieve a goal, we are acting as leaders. We have been leaders in the past and we will continue to be leaders in the future. Our only question is whether we want to improve our effectiveness in leading others by following the true master leader.

Jesus and his followers changed the history of the world. Reading the story of his perfect leadership example reveals that Jesus succeeded by empowering his disciples with great faith and confidence in accomplishing the work at hand. This endowment of power and understanding not only produced magnificent achievement in his immediate disciples but in their successors as well.

Like the early followers of Christ, we have the same opportunity to realize our own leadership potentials. Elder Neal A. Maxwell testifies that Jesus is "the perfect Example and Leader, not asking us to do what he has not done, not asking us to endure what he has not endured, giving us enough, but not more than we can manage. I thank him who did everything perfectly for sharing his precious work with those of us who then do it so imperfectly. I testify that he and the Father are serious about stretching our souls in this second estate. I thank him for truly teaching us about our personal possibilities and for divinely demonstrating directions—not just pointing" (Maxwell, 1976, 27).

We Grow through Daily Experiences

Christ's disciples had difficulty, early in their ministry, trying to follow the example of their great leader. The scriptures record an incident in which the early disciples were not able to heal a young man who was foaming at the mouth and gnashing his teeth. Jesus reproved the disciples for their lack of faith. He then healed the youth and later instructed his disciples: "This kind can come forth by nothing but prayer and fasting" (Mark 9:14–29).

Later, as these same disciples continued to grow and develop, they gained the faith and confidence necessary to heal a man who was lame since birth. Peter and John said, "In the name of Jesus of Nazareth rise and walk." Immediately, the man stood up and started walking and leaping, praising God (see Acts 3:1–7).

We all accept our leadership opportunities with considerable fear and trembling. Sleepless nights often follow the calling of a new Relief Society leader or quorum president. General authorities of the Church are not immune to the feeling of weakness, especially when they contemplate the extent of their new responsibilities.

Most parents constantly worry about how well they lead their children and whether they are effectively influencing their children toward a wholesome life. We become great leaders and valued friends by exerting a strong positive influence in our families, church callings, and work activities. Consequently, we need to follow more closely the example of Jesus as he attempted to influence, lead, and change people's lives for the better.

Jesus is the cornerstone of religious conviction. A person untouched by the words and deeds of Christ lacks the element that engenders great and noble leadership. We need constantly to keep Jesus in the foreground of our daily living. We need to let him be the light by which we see the way. Each of us must reflect the remarkable attributes of

Jesus by adopting his words and deeds in our own lives. Thus as Jesus lived and led so must we also live and lead.

In these pages, we have attempted to illuminate the essence of Jesus' leadership through his deeds and teachings. Five quintessential keys to powerful leadership have been identified and discussed.

These keys can serve as a guide to personal growth. For example, young people can retain these principles in their minds and let the principles guide them as they grow into leadership roles. These keys can balance their lives and eliminate incongruities between how they act at work, home, and church. As a way to keep hopes and dreams alive, Jesus' leadership approach represents a tried and true way to succeed.

For those who now occupy leadership positions, these five keys might indicate areas of weakness where a little improvement might result in big gains. Our experience with leaders is that many have unknowingly overlooked some of the most sublime principles associated with true leadership.

Should you decide to accept the challenge of being a more effective leader and start adding to your present leadership abilities, you will want to consider these final suggestions.

Treat Others as Friends

The greatest gift we can give ourselves is to become transformed into Christ's friends, as his earlier followers did. The greatest gift we can give others is to help them become similarly transformed.

If we let Jesus' words abide in us, love one another, and follow his perfect leadership example, we can have the ennobling experiences that he had and become his friends. Then we can go forward as the Savior did and help to heal and transform others. "Herein," says Jesus, "is my Father glorified, that ye bear much fruit: so shall ye be my disciple" (John 15:8).

When we genuinely treat others as friends, they tend to like us and be influenced by what we say and do. Hence, treating others as friends enhances our leadership effectiveness.

Hostility between managers and followers is much too prevalent in the workplace. Informed and knowledgeable workers usually view traditional leaders and managers negatively. Workers frequently consider traditional leadership behaviors as demeaning to their abilities.

Under such management approaches, workers become alienated and passive. They withhold their insights and observations and play political games. Everyone suffers, and the organization itself loses strength and vitality.

Most of this workplace hostility comes about because of a poor relationship between the leader and the people over whom he or she has some authority. Edward L. Moyers, CEO of Illinois Central Railroad, gave this advice to those who aspire to be successful mangers and leaders:

> Take time to visit with those people at every level in your organization. The increased production, improvement in morale, and verbal support that you will receive as the result of such activities is amazing. Take enough time with those who report directly to you to determine what motivates them. Have a clear understanding with everyone as to his or her objectives.
>
> Take care of the employees who report to you—salary, recognition, awards, et cetera. After all, these are the people who have made you a success and they are the people who will insure your future success. You have a lot in common with these people. They are depending on you and you are depending on them. (Speech given to Millsaps College Commencement, Jackson, Mississippi, May 13, 2000)

If You Push Hard, They Will Push Back

The above statement actually encapsulates the final result of a massive research program aimed at finding better ways to improve the relationship between parents and children. If the parents threaten, coerce, and are too authoritative with their children, the report said, the children start to rebel, threaten their parents, and become more disobedient. The whole idea for improving parent-child relationships is to mutually decide on the rules of the house, mutually try to agree on family goals, and mutually discuss family problems and challenges in order to find acceptable solutions. The children need maximum support, which means that parents not only need to make friends with their own children but also with the friends of their children. Parents should always celebrate small wins and victories with their children so that everyone feels the excitement of accomplishing good things.

The same general principle holds true for management and leadership in the workplace. If you push people too hard, they will push back. On the contrary, if you demonstrate sensitivity, show empathy, and exhibit patience, your employees will be more supportive toward you. If your relationship with employees goes well, usually the work goes well.

Don't try to manipulate people and impress them. Rather, treat them as friends, and show respect for them by asking for their ideas to make things better. Think more about how to make heroes out of your children and fellow employees than to make a hero out of yourself.

Create a Positive Force

Good leaders are never dull. They create a feeling that things are moving in a positive way. They demonstrate by their walk and their talk that they are filled with quiet confidence and great strength. They unleash the total power of their personalities.

Each of us must develop our own positive force. Like the Savior, we need to decide to what things we will be enthusiastically committed, see that followers are treated compassionately, and lead with encouragement and a positive attitude.

Sister Carmen Sanchez was called to be a Relief Society leader in a university ward. She was young, somewhat inexperienced, and very nervous about the calling. During the first meeting, attendance was low and the young ladies who did attend did not respond well to the lesson.

Carmen was determined, however, to make things better. She committed herself to making her Relief Society the best in the Stake. She became friends with all the members. She talked with them about their needs and about their future aspirations. She made her comments positive and encouraging.

Sister Sanchez soon built a loving relationship with each member of the Relief Society. The young sisters began to attend meetings and became more involved in the lessons. Carmen didn't understand all the principles that contribute to effective leadership but she did create a positive force.

Preserve Others Confidence in Themselves

The boldness and power of Jesus' leadership was always tempered by a genuine concern for the feelings and needs of others. A person's self-concept and self-esteem are terribly fragile entities and require a considerable amount of nurturing and gentle development. Most of us feel degraded, rejected, and incapable of coping when our behaviors are criticized.

Frequently leaders tend to fall into the criticism trap when they try to correct the mistakes made by those over whom they have some responsibility or influence. Because leaders play such an important role in the happiness, vitality, and confidence of followers, adopting a way to correct mistakes without criticism is very important in the workplace, in the family, and in the church.

The safest route to take in correcting others is to use the skill called *redirection*. The process of redirecting people involves getting them to acknowledge that they have deviated from acceptable performance or behavior and then to help them understand how a change might be made to get back on the right track. The redirection process consists of four rather simple steps:

1. Awareness. Help individuals recognize what they are doing that is causing problems. Ask them simple questions in a friendly way. If necessary, give them information you have received about the problem behavior, and ask them if they are aware of what is happening. Don't make any judgments; just ask questions.

2. Consequences. Ask them what they are trying to achieve in the particular situation under discussion. If necessary, clarify with them what will probably happen if the behavior continues.

3. Decision to Change. Ask the individual if there is anything they would like to change in their current behavior to make things better or to avoid some of the eventual consequences. If it seems appropriate, or if an individual asks about various options, offer examples of what others have done. The important thing here is to let the individual decide how to make things better. When you jump in with all your great wisdom, your suggestions tend to fit no one but you. Each of us is different. What works for one may not work for another. Also, we seldom know the unique strengths and capabilities of other people, especially those with whom we work. Let them play to their own strengths, and they will probably succeed.

4. Support the Decision. This is the step that creates a wonderful enabling, energizing, and positive feeling in the individual that you are redirecting. Once the person has made a decision to change for the better, offer your help in every way possible to facilitate the change and to reinforce the desired behavior. Encourage and energize the individual by pointing out the benefits of the change. Then, express personal confidence in the person's ability to move ahead in the decision. Don't forget to provide an opportunity for the person to return and report on successful progress so you can celebrate together.

Always be positive and encouraging when you are leading others. Avoid criticism and judgment, increase applauding and celebrating successes. Eliminate using words that put people on the defensive.

Avoid saying "Why didn't you?" "You should have . . ." "You must never . . ." "If you had only . . ." "Don't you understand that . . . ?" Most people perceive these phrases as criticisms. Notice that each phrase implies a judgment.

At work, use optimistic words to communicate and interact with others from morning until evening. At home, the same thing should happen. When you communicate with others in an understanding, informative, and friendly way, relationships are strengthened, people feel supported and you have created a strong positive force in others.

When leaders fail to create a strong force, lethargy usually sets in among their followers. Unfortunately, people follow the path of least resistance, slow down, and quickly become disenchanted. Being positive and encouraging when things are not going well is difficult. Effective leaders, however, have no other choice.

Invite Others to Follow

If there are no followers, there is no leader. A leader may want to lead, and even be appointed to lead, but the ability to attract followers initially determines whether the leader will be successful.

Leadership theories assume that if we want to attract followers, we must prepare ourselves to inspire them by creating an attractive vision of what can be achieved, and motivate them by continuously and vividly showing that vision. Finally, the leader confidently invites others to unite in achieving the vision.

All of us like to follow leaders who have made the kind of achievements we would like to make, and who rejoice in their accomplishments. Christ spent his whole life describing a joyful lifestyle that helps lighten the burdens of mankind. Faith, repentance, baptism, and the gift of the Holy Ghost were the messages he exhorted over and over to everyone who would listen.

"Come, follow me," Jesus implored. I am the light, the living water, the way. He urged us to be perfect as our Father in Heaven is perfect. He wanted us to have the power to do the things that he did. The vision that Jesus presents to people is magnificent. Millions are attracted to him and his ideas.

Goals help us implement our vision. Goals are statements of what needs to be done to achieve the vision. One way to create a goal is to identify a concern that is bothersome or uncomfortable. Attempt to think of something about your family that is of concern to you. You might think that your family members are *not kind enough to one another*. In other words, you may feel uncomfortable that family members do not show kindness often enough to one another.

Next, turn your concern into a goal by deciding, with your spouse and children, what each individual family member should do to show more kindness to family members. Each person in the family, for example, might compliment, do an act of service, or give a gift to another family member sometime during the next month. Now, the concern has been turned into a goal by making a statement of what you would do to alleviate the concern. Giving a small gift shows kindness, thus your goal is to have everyone give someone else a gift.

The very same procedure can be used in the business world. Say to yourself, "Right now, my main concern with the company is that we are not providing adequate customer service." Once again, decide, with the help of other employees, how to overcome your concern. The answer will be a goal that will eliminate the concern and lead the company to achieve the vision.

How would you translate that concern into a goal? Yes! That is correct! The goal might read: Each employee will perform one or more acts of customer service each day.

Your next step is to invite as many people as possible to be involved in achieving the goal. Then do what the Savior did: Speak and instruct with great diligence and patience until everyone understands. Be sure to ask questions to confirm their understanding and listen to questions to confirm your own understanding.

As with Jesus, if our goals, dreams, and visions are attractive to people, they will want to join in and reap the rewards.

Enable Followers to Act

Have you ever had the experience of telling a child, "Immediately after family home evening, we are going to bake some delicious chocolate chip cookies?" After the closing prayer, with a twinkle in her eye and grinning ear to ear, she dashes into the kitchen. She can already taste the warm cookies melting in her mouth. But usually, in less than a minute, she is back, realizing that she doesn't know where to begin or what to do. The goal was clear, but its implementation could not occur until more specific details were given.

Lofty goals without ways to achieve them are not useful. Individuals must be invited to participate, then instructed in how to become involved in achieving the goals.

First, delegate activities that lead to the accomplishment of the goals. Give each person a specific assignment. Discuss the best ways to do the assignment so that it will most likely be completed. Ask each individual to describe what should be done, and when.

Second, invite all persons, individually, to begin; express your appreciation for their involvement and willingness to accept the assignment. Indicate how soon the assignment needs to be completed, and have them give you a progress report. Do not be afraid to encourage them to take full responsibility for seeing that the assignment is completed on time.

When disapproval needs to be expressed, do it with charity, clarity, and specificity. Focus on aspects of the assignment that were not completed, rather than on the person. Show forth an increase in love toward the person reproved (see D&C 121:43).

The leader's task is to involve as many people as possible. Everyone should do something in order to feel the excitement and share the thrill of successfully completing a project. But it is not enough to invite people to be involved or to delegate a task to each individual to complete.

An effective leader enables followers to act by sharing information about how others have previously tried to accomplish a particular task. This avoids wasteful duplication and even total failure.

Even with something as basic as home teaching and visiting teaching, your followers need to understand how the most successful home and visiting teaching have been accomplished. Your home and visiting teachers may need to understand the concept of "watching over others" to even begin to understand how to carry out their assignments.

Another good way to enable people to solve a problem or carry out an assignment effectively is to encourage them to ask coworkers what they would suggest doing to resolve the problem or to carry out an assignment or task. People feel more confident when they receive support and ideas from their colleagues about how to proceed.

The last goal of leaders in enabling others to carry out the work is to let them know what the expectations are with regards to the work or assignment. Again, referring to home teaching, be sure that everyone is clear on when the initial visit to the family is to be completed and what kind of dress is appropriate. Then consider what temporal and spiritual welfare inquiries need to be made in the home, how much time should be spent in the home, and should there be a prayer? You might consider giving a Priesthood blessing, and, finally, be clear about who the home teacher should report to when the assignment is completed.

Providing information, resources and expectations help people perform at their highest levels. We have all heard the old saying that goes like this: Success breeds success. We have all experienced the power of this simple statement. When we succeed in doing something, and doing it well, we feel enthusiastic and stimulated to try it again or enlarge upon our success. Enabling people frees them up for success. You may have to spend a little time instructing and training people, but whatever it takes will be worth it for you as a leader.

Enabling people requires that you always know what they are doing and staying close to them. You should emulate Christ's example by not being afraid to eat, walk, work, and laugh together, as friends, with those whom you are asked to lead.

Strengthen Yourself
It is not easy to be positive and enthusiastic as we attempt to lead others.

To follow the example of him who constantly encouraged us to "be of good cheer" can be accomplished only if we pay proper attention to our sources of physical and spiritual strength. Physical fitness is a subject of prominent interest in countries all around the world. Physiologists unanimously agree that regular exercise tends to help people respond better to everyday stresses.

A good conditioning program for most people should raise the heart beat above 100 beats per minute for twenty to thirty minutes, three or four times a week. Brisk walking, jogging, cycling, dancing, swimming, and participating in a competitive sport are all useful ways of strengthening our bodies.

All the benefits of regular exercise are reduced considerably without good nutrition, and proper rest. We also need to avoid harmful substances like caffeine, nicotine, alcohol, and all mind-and-emotion-altering drugs.

Leaders should not only get appropriate exercise, rest, and nutrition, but they should also develop a balanced pattern of living. Overly tense people and workaholics tend to have more health problems, especially heart disease. Perhaps the Savior's example of walking outdoors, and engaging in social, family, intellectual, and spiritual activities, is a good one for us to follow.

The goal, remember, is not to compound problems by adding more undertakings to our already busy lives, but to develop a better balance among our daily activities. Realizing that we can't do everything that we would like to do for our family, friends, and fellow workers, we must prioritize a little and probably let a number of "would like to do's" left undone. Former President Harold B. Lee gives us great insight into how to balance our lives and schedule our time:

> Most men do not set priorities to guide them in allocating their time, and most men forget that the first priority should be to maintain their own spiritual and physical strength. Then comes their family, then the church, and then their professions—and all need time.

Notice that the first priority is to strengthen yourself spiritually and physically. That is, if you are weak spiritually and lack faith and confidence in what you are doing, and if you are weak physically, you will have great difficulty trying to lead and encourage others.

Spiritual strength comes from exercising our faith in the Jesus and applying it to an important work or calling. A speck of faith, like a mustard seed, can control and calm adverse circumstances that impede our progress toward worthy goals.

Great spiritual strength comes through prayer, keeping the commandments, and being sensitive to the still small voice of the Spirit. This Divine form of communication is critical in learning how to lead like Jesus, because we know that He left neither detailed rules nor ready references to be used in all leadership situations.

President Benson reminds us that "usually the Lord gives us the overall objectives to be accomplished and some guidelines to follow, but he expects us to work out most of the details and methods. The methods and procedures are usually developed through study and prayer and by living so that we can obtain and follow the promptings of the Spirit" (Benson, April 1965).

Imagine with us now that it is early morning, and the sun is just beginning to glitter on the surface of the sea as the men strain to cast nets into the water. Beads of perspiration appear on their foreheads as they toil. A lone, solitary figure strolls along the shore, intently studying their activities. As he nears their place of work, he says, "Hello, Peter and Andrew. I am in need of good men to assist in the work of the Gospel. Follow me, and I will make you fishers of men." They immediately dropped their nets and followed him.

Without hesitation, they followed Jesus, as we may also. They shared in his vision of eternal life. They grew by his constant direction and drew from his boundless energy. They were enlivened by his conviction and dynamic communication, as well as ennobled by his patient and enduring instruction. As leaders, we must do the same.

The coming decade promises great challenges and opportunities for us in every leadership responsibility. Elder John E. Carmack, former executive director of the Church Historical Department, observed that "the Church and individuals will thrive if they turn problems into opportunities and grow. We will need to be careful of our resources, simplify our procedures, have more independence, and do things of our own free will and choice" (Van Orden and Avant, 7).

With the help of our Lord and Savior, we will meet our challenges and unparalleled opportunities as mothers and fathers, as teachers and leaders in this remarkable era. Though the tempests rage about us, and the waves crest and fall, let us courageously follow the example of Jesus. Let us hear again in our own hearts, as his faithful followers heard it on the Sea of Galilee, the voice of the Master whispering to us, "It is I, Jesus. Be not afraid."

7

CHURCH LEADERS ON LEADERSHIP

W e would like you to read what four Church leaders have to say about principles of effective leadership. You can find these articles on the Internet at http://lds.org or in the Church magazines that we have referenced.

Elder Joseph B. Wirthlin of the Quorum of the Twelve Apostles, in "Guided by His Exemplary Life" (*Ensign*, September 1995, 32), explains some singularly important leadership acts of Jesus and relates them to our own leadership efforts.

President N. Eldon Tanner, former first counselor in the First Presidency, states that "Everyone is a leader or has influence in the lives of others even though he may not realize it" ("Leading as the Savior Led," *New Era*, June 1977, 4). President Tanner raises the questions, "What kind of leader will we be?" and "What kind of influence will we have?"

President Spencer W. Kimball points out a few attributes and skills that Jesus demonstrated so perfectly and that are important for us all if we wish to succeed as leaders in any lasting way (Sun Valley, Idaho, January 15, 1977; also *Ensign*, August 1979, 5).

President James E. Faust, second counselor in the First Presidency, points out various principles and skills that make leadership function effectively in the Church ("These I Will Make My Leaders," *Ensign*, November 1980, 34).

What makes a successful leader? Are powerful leaders born? If they are not born, then how do they grow and develop to become a powerful influence in their families, among their friends and associates, and at their places of work? What combination of skills do these leaders use to unite their followers and focus their performance on the achievement of the highest goals?

As you assimilate what each Church leader says, notice the various circumstances from which they each articulate their experience. Also, be sensitive to the excellent examples of the five powerful leadership keys that each of these leaders present as they encourage us to become better leaders.

References

Benson, Ezra Taft. In Conference Report, April 1965.

———. In Conference Report, October 1974.

Book of Mormon. Translated by Joseph Smith. Salt Lake City, Utah: The Church of Jesus Christ of Latter-day Saints, 1981.

BYU Today. Provo, Utah: Brigham Young University, November 1989.

Editors of *Campus Life* magazine. *Reach Out*. Wheaton, Ill.: Tyndale House Foundation, 1967.

Faust, James E. "These I Will Make My Leaders." *Ensign*, November 1980, 34; or at http://lds.org (accessed November 3, 2006).

Gospel Doctrine. 5th ed. Salt Lake City: Deseret Book, 1939.

Holy Bible. Authorized King James Version. Salt Lake City, Utah: The Church of Jesus Christ of Latter-day Saints, 1979.

Kimball, Spencer W. "The Perfect Executive." Address given to the Young Presidents organization, Sun Valley, Idaho, January 15, 1977.

———. "Jesus: The Perfect Leader." *Ensign*, August 1979, 5; or at http://lds.org (accessed November 3, 2006).

Lee, Harold B. Address to LDS seminary and institute teachers, Brigham Young University, Provo, Utah, July 6, 1956.

Leslie, Robert C. *Jesus and Logotherapy.* Nashville, Tenn.: Abingdon Press, 1965.

Maxwell, Neal A. "Jesus of Nazareth, Savior and King." *Ensign*, March, 1976.

McKay, David O. *Gospel Ideals.* Salt Lake City, Utah: *Improvement Era*, 1953.

———. *Man May Know For Himself.* Compiled by Clare Middlemiss. Salt Lake City, Utah: Deseret Book, 1969.

Melchizedek Priesthood Personal Study Guide 1989. Salt Lake City, Utah: The Church of Jesus Christ of Latter-day Saints, 1988.

Romney, Marion G. "What Would Jesus Do?" *New Era*, September, 1972.

Smith, Joseph. Doctrine and Covenants. Salt Lake City, Utah: The Church of Jesus Christ of Latter-day Saints, 1974.

———. *Lectures on Faith.* Salt Lake City: Deseret Book, 1985.

———. *Teachings of the Prophet Joseph Smith.* Selected by Joseph Fielding Smith. Salt Lake City, Utah: Deseret Press, 1938.

Talmage, James E. *Jesus The Christ.* Salt Lake City, Utah: Deseret Book, 1973.

Tanner, N. Eldon. "Leading as the Savior Led," *New Era*, June 1977, 4; or at http://lds.org (accessed November 3, 2006).

———. "The Message." *New Era*, June, 1977.

Van Orden, Dell and Gerry Avant. "Church Gears Up," *Deseret News: LDS Church News*, January 13, 1990.

Wirthlin, Joseph B. "Guided by His Exemplary Life." Ensign, September 1995, 32; or at http://lds.org (accessed November 3, 2006).

Index

Love in leadership, 14–15

Maxwell, Neal A., 83–84
McKay, David O.: on being
    Christlike, 6; on friendship,
    10–11; on being receptive to
    the Spirit, 74–75
Mission statements, 39
Mothers, working, 79. *See also*
    Parents as leaders

Nelson, Russell M., 42–43

Packer, Boyd K., patience of, 46
Parents as leaders, 40–41. *See
    also* Children, taking time for;
    Family
Patience in leadership, 45–46
Physical health, 63–66
Positive image, creating a, 87
Prayer: strengthening ourselves
    through, 92–95; Christ finds
    strength in, 71–72
Pythias and Damon, 9–10

Questions, leaders must prepare
    for, 43–45

Romney, Marion G., 72

Scriptures, leadership taught in, 3
Service: leading through, 13,
    21–22; joy in, 82
Smith, Joseph: on friendship, 11;
    on faith, 70
Spirit of the law, 76–79
Spiritual health, 66, 93–94

Talmage, James E.: on body of
    Christ, 63; on faith, 70–71
Tanner, N. Eldon: everyone is a
    leader, 97; as Christ led, refer
    to http://lds.org
Temptations, facing, 18–20

Visionary aspect of leadership,
    36–37

Wells, John, 74–75
Wirthlin, Joseph B.: exemplary
    life, Christ's, refer to http://lds.
    org
Word of Wisdom, 64–66. *See also*
    Health
Working mothers, 79. *See also*
    Parents as leaders

Eric G. Stephan

E ric G. Stephan is a professor emeritus of organizational leadership at Brigham Young University. A popular speaker and author, he has made presentations at BYU Campus Education Week and at Know Your Religion programs throughout the United States.

Eric has served as a high councilor, bishop, branch president, and stake executive secretary. He and his wife, Sandra, are the parents of seven children and the grandparents of a group of wonderful grandchildren.

R. Wayne Pace

Wayne Pace, professor emeritus of organizational leadership at Brigham Young University, has served as president of the Academy of Human Resource Development and of the International Communication Association.

Wayne has served as a high councilor, stake director of teacher development, and counselor in a bishopric. He and his wife, Gae, are the parents of six children, several grandchildren, and a few great-grandchildren.